Single Dose

Single Dose

Finding Peace, Fulfillment, and Contentment Being Single

April Harding

Abundant Publishing

Dallas, Texas

Single Dose
Finding Peace, Fulfillment, and Contentment
Being Single

ISBN: 978-1-7334011-9-7 (Paperback)

ASIN: B07HMLKY5X (eBook)

Printed in the United States of America

Author photograph by Lawrence Jenkins

Editing by Michelle Chester www.ebm-services.com

For Chari'

To my daughter, the sweetest young lady in the whole wide world and joy of my life. You are the most important thing in the world to me. Thank you for being my joy during the tough times. I hope and pray that you will live life to the fullest whether you are married or single.

I love you.

Contents

Acknowledgments

❧ ◆ ❧

Scott Harris, who motivated me to publish this book, Robin Marlowe, who inspired me to reach for my potential, Mary Goin, who encouraged me to allow my true personality to show, Zelma Batie, who challenged me to always strive for the best, Vera Andrews, who showed me how to have courage and accountability, and my mom, Othella Brown, the sweetest person I know, who taught me how to pray consistently. From my heart, thank you.

Introduction

For years I have met so many divorced singles whose lives are stagnant because they are still holding on to the past. They refuse to let go of what has happened. Others are just waiting for the next person to come along in hope that life will get better for them. They've put their lives on hold, hoping to find Mr. or Ms. Right. I wrote *Single Dose* to help singles everywhere move past a static position in life and on to finding how sweet life can be.

With the rise of divorce, more and more people are becoming single. Whether single by divorce, death, choice, or just not having met that special someone yet, there are many people who are living the single life.

After my divorce, I had a hard time finding the help I needed. I looked everywhere. I found encouragement in some books but couldn't find everything in one place. I did find answers, however, for every challenge I had, in the Bible. I studied the Bible to see what God's word has to say about relationships, marriage, and divorce. I began to write notes of instruction for myself. I kept a journal about every emotion and phase I experienced during the divorce. Anytime something would come up that I needed help with, I would search the scriptures.

During my prayer time with God, I would write messages with which He inspired me and encouraged my heart. I would write them down and then read them for encouragement. I would wake up in the middle of the night and write notes of encouragement that came to me.

In desperate times when I needed counsel and didn't know where to turn, I would write letters to myself asking for advice. Then I would step out of the scenario and answer the letters as if I were someone else. I did this because I felt I didn't have anywhere else to turn and didn't know who to talk to. I thought by stepping out of the problem and looking at it objectively, as if I were someone else, I could be more honest with myself. This technique helped a lot.

I conducted research by talking to other singles about how they felt about being single. I took informal surveys with other divorced singles about their experience and the aftermath of divorce. I gained a lot of knowledge and insight by talking to people about various relationships.

Through my own experience and observations, I have discovered similarities in actions, reactions, and circumstances. Based on what I've observed, I have written, tried, and proven some practical steps and fundamental rules for how to approach single life. As an instructional designer, I write classroom curriculum, online courses, and operational procedures to facilitate learning. I applied my writing skills to develop practical steps and guidance for approaching some of the more common areas singles face. I attempted to capture every circumstance, challenge, and emotion I experienced personally and noted in others and tried to put the lessons learned in writing to demonstrate how to let go of the past and enjoy life as a single.

This is not a venue to whine, complain, or air dirty laundry. There is no male bashing here. There is only practical and candid advice to show singles how to enjoy life.

Single Dose is for men and women. The topics covered are common for each. Because of this I try to address men and women by writing "he" in one sentence and "she" in the next. *Single Dose* is for those who are single because of divorce, who have never been married, who are widowed, or who simply choose not to marry. The first few chapters are for those who are divorced. The remaining chapters are for those who are single for other reasons.

As a Christian believer, I have written *Single Dose* from a Christian perspective with what some may consider aggressive principles. For example, the chapter on sexual temptation suggests some strong methods for avoiding compromising situations. You may ask, *Is it realistic? Is it necessary?* The answer is– any type of growth takes time. We will never attain perfection, naturally speaking. However, we can take life one day at a time and allow God to help us live to our individual potential. Part of living a fulfilling single life includes making the sacrifices necessary on a daily basis, yet still enjoying good times.

There have been times in my life when it was difficult for me to be happy or content. I have struggled with loneliness, sexual temptation, poor money management, and doubt about who I am and what my purpose is. Over time, however, I have learned many valuable lessons. I have learned how to manage myself in these areas in order to live a life of peace with myself and gain respect from others. I have found how knowing my purpose brings a greater sense of completeness than anything or anyone could ever give. I'm not perfect. I still make mistakes, but I take life one day at a time and I consciously allow God to help me do the things I need to do on a daily basis.

I frequently revisit *Single Dose*, as it has become an antidote for any discontentment I occasionally feel in my life. At times when I feel that desperate yearning for companionship, I pick up *Single Dose* to remind myself of what I need to do to maintain peace of mind and happiness with where I am in my life right now.

My hope and prayer are that *Single Dose* will enlighten you on some of the issues you may face. In each chapter, you will see steps to follow to help you practice the concepts provided. You'll also have the opportunity to answer questions at the end of each chapter to reflect on how you are progressing in different areas. Be honest with yourself as you read and think about each question.

If you're not single because of divorce, you may read the first chapter and then skip to the chapter on loneliness.

Find a quiet place where you can sit, relax, and slowly soak up these words. I promise you'll find a single dose of peace and fulfillment for your life as you read.

CHAPTER 1

Changing Your Mind-Set

ɚ◆ɕ

Most of the singles I've talked to throughout the years are pretty content with being single. Most have established a good lifestyle being alone. Some have bought their own house and their own car. They have investments and a retirement plan. I would say many singles are satisfied living alone.

On the other hand, there are other singles who have not yet learned how to be content living alone. They are still searching for something or someone to make them happy. They are still waiting for that spouse before they buy their dream house. There are some singles who are sitting around moping about not being married.

It took me approximately two years after divorce to get to a place where I was content with being single. It took a while to get past the emotional grief of divorce. In general, I enjoy marriage and the whole idea of sharing life with someone forever, so it was difficult for me to adjust to the thought of being alone for the rest of my life.

A counselor once told me that divorce actually happens in a person's heart long before the separation and actual divorce occurs. Divorce usually starts with a "distant" feeling and behavior between husband and wife. Because of this, there's a long stretch of time when we experience a feeling of emptiness, starting before the divorce and continuing afterward. It takes a while to move from those emotional ups and downs to a level of security and contentment with one's life.

I'm the type of person who questions everything. I had many questions about my marriage and the divorce. I tried to figure things out in my head. I often wondered what I could have done to save the marriage. So, you see, I had a lot of "stuff" to move past before I could accept that I was now single again.

Even if you have never been married, you may still have emotional ups and downs. There will be times you're glad to be single and other times when you long to be with someone. Sometimes you will talk to

1

married people about their problems and be glad you're not married. Other times you will see happy couples and wish that was you.

Feelings of contentment come and go. There are happy times and lonely times. There is a way to have a consistent sense of fulfillment, though. That sense of fulfillment and contentment begins with your frame of mind. It begins with you being comfortable with who you are and loving yourself. It comes with being thankful for whatever place you are in your life. It comes with setting goals for yourself and actively reaching toward those goals daily.

When you know who you are, accept who you are, and love who you are, you will feel better about where you are in your life. When you set goals and find yourself accomplishing those goals, you will feel a greater sense of completeness with each success.

Change your frame of mind from "waiting" to "doing." Stop waiting for life to happen for you. Start doing something to make life happen. Don't sit around waiting for someone to enter your life to make you happy. Take the steps necessary to make yourself happy. Change your perspective from that of a hopeless single person to that of an ambitious complete person. Be ambitious by seeking opportunities to make life better for yourself. Do what you need to do to gain more energy and momentum in your life.

I've dealt with many issues as a single person. I failed many times in several areas before realizing what the antidote was. I consider myself a strong person emotionally, but there were times when I fell to the floor in my living room and cried my heart out. Life hurts sometimes. I never will forget, though, the moment I found contentment with my life. I walked into my house one day and it hit me. I said to myself, "Wow, I love being single right now. I am happy with my life." At that moment, I realized how good I had it. No, everything was not perfect. I still had bills to pay. I still struggled with loneliness every now and then. But at that very moment, I realized that I have a pretty good life. I have peace of mind, and that feels so good. There is no drama in my life, and that feels great. I know who I am and accept my personality; and that feels wonderful.

Sometimes we can get so busy that we forget who we are and why we are here. We forget to take the time to show love to others. We're so worried about finding someone and getting married that we forget to be who we are right now and use what we have right now to reach out to others. We are so consumed with work and other activities that we forget to be who we are and enjoy life.

Look at your life and find out who you are. What are your attributes? What are you good at? What do you enjoy doing? What are your dreams and goals? What areas in your life do you need to improve? Change your focus to enjoying life. Forget about the past. Let go of any bad feelings you might have in your heart towards anyone. Concentrate on living life to the fullest right now.

As you reach for your goals, you will feel better and better. In time, you will gain a sense of contentment and fulfillment. The feelings of emptiness will one day be replaced with a sense of completeness. Even though you will continue to reach for goals, you will be satisfied with your life. If you find yourself feeling discontent and unfulfilled, change your perspective.

Start thinking more positively about your life. Think about the good things you have. Focus on what's good about being single. Just for fun, and to help you think about the positive side of being single, I've listed ten reasons it's great to be single. Revisit this list when you feel down and remind yourself of how good you really have it.

See yourself as an empowered individual who has control of his or her life. Seek to do whatever you need to do to enjoy life. Get rid of whatever is holding you back from enjoying life. Don't let people drain your energy to do the things you want to do. Take the steps now to change your way of thinking about being single and enjoy your life.

Ten Reasons It's Great to Be Single

1. You have more time to serve at church and in the community.
2. You can focus on your career.
3. You have the freedom to make your own decisions.
4. You can manage your money the way you want.
5. You have the freedom to come and go as you please.
6. You can relax after work without having to cook dinner when you don't feel like it.
7. You have more time to develop friendships and relationships.
8. You can watch your own favorite television shows and listen to your own favorite radio stations.
9. You only have one set of laundry and dishes, and less cleaning to do.
10. You look better because you get more rest and able to spend more money on grooming.

How to Change Your Mind-Set

1. **Make a list of all the things in your life for which you are grateful.** This list will serve as a reminder that you have something to be thankful for. It will make you feel better to think about what's positive in your life. Look back over your life and write things that you have accomplished. Some of the things on my list are "no drama in my life," "a sweet daughter," "a good job," "good health," and "peaceful home." When I feel down, I look at my list. It makes me smile and wipes away all feelings of discontentment. You can list people in your life who are a positive influence. You can list things that are of value to you. When you finish the list, put it in a place where you can access it quickly and easily. This list will remind you of how good your life is. Add to the list as time progresses.

2. **Move out of the "waiting" mode.** If you are waiting for marriage to reach for certain goals, stop waiting. You might eventually marry. However, don't put life on hold to wait for a spouse. Enjoy life now. Accomplish the things you want to accomplish now. You may just meet a potential spouse in the process. If you want to buy a house, go ahead and do that. If you want to wait for a spouse before buying a house because you feel you may need a bigger house, go ahead and buy a house that fits your budget now. You and your spouse could buy a bigger house if needed. Be open to the possibilities of life as a single person. You don't have to be married to pursue your dreams.

3. **Take care of yourself.** We often burden ourselves as singles by taking care of everyone else in our life and not taking care of ourselves. Sometimes people around us tend to think we have more time and availability because we are single, so they bombard us with requests for favors. We give all our money to our children, we spend our free time babysitting our grandchildren, we're at the church every night of the week, and we work sixty to seventy hours a week. We don't allow time to take care of ourselves.

I am not saying we should not help others. The most important thing we are to do in life is to love others. However, don't neglect yourself by overspending your time taking care of everyone else. Commit some time each day (or week) to you. Spend some time doing things just for yourself. Treat yourself to a massage. Sleep extra late on your off days. Take a nap every now and then.

Eat healthy, balanced meals. Don't allow your friends, family, job, or church obligations to drain your energy and money. Create balance in your life by giving to God first, loving your friends and family, and then committing time to take care of yourself and enjoy life.

4. **Get rid of the "victim" mentality and be honest with yourself and others.** I know a lady who constantly complains about doing favors for her family and friends. The people around her always seem to need her assistance in some way or another. Every time I talk to her, she complains about helping people and how tired she is of doing so. From what she says the requests are sometimes unreasonable favors.

One day as I was listening to her complain, I wondered why she continued to allow people to take advantage of her. Then one day I heard somebody say something that made me think of her. He said that some people have a "victim" mentality. Those with a "victim" mentality continually allow negative things to happen to them because they *want* to feel like a victim. It makes them feel accepted and makes others feel sorry for them. It's not something they consciously do, but it happens.

If you are doing unreasonable favors for others and find yourself resenting them and complaining about them, stop doing those favors. You are not acting in love if you are grudgingly giving to others. Also, you are not being honest with yourself or with them. Learn how to say "no." People will appreciate and respect your honesty if you lovingly let them know that you are not able to do what they are asking. Respecting others by being honest with them is part of living a fulfilling single life. It involves taking care of yourself. It means you'll have more peace with yourself, because you are only doing what you are able to do within reason without sacrificing your peace of mind and life balance. Empower yourself to be a strong and independent single person. Take charge of your life. Don't let others manipulate your time, money, or energy.

Don't have a "victim" mentality. People will accept you and love you for who you are without having to feel sorry for you.

Scriptures for Changing Your Mind-Set

Matthew 6:34 Therefore do not worry about tomorrow, for tomorrow will worry about itself. Each day has enough trouble of its own.

2 Corinthians 9:7 Each man should give what he has decided in his heart to give, not reluctantly or under compulsion, for God loves a cheerful giver.

Proverbs 24:26 An honest answer is like a kiss on the lips.

Hebrews 13:5 Let your conduct be without covetousness; be content with such things as you have. For he himself has said, "I will never leave you nor forsake you." (KJV)

Prayer for Changing My Mind-Set

Lord, as you know, I am not content with my life right now. I'm not happy about being single. I desire companionship. I don't feel like doing a whole lot with my life right now. I'm wondering if you're ever going to send me a mate. Lord, please give me strength and peace of mind. Help me to be content with my life.

Show me what you would have me to do to help others. I want to share with others out of love and not out of obligation. Show me how to do that. Help me walk in honesty with everyone. Show me how to love my friends and family without draining all my energy.

I know you created me for a reason, and I ask that you reveal my purpose so I can live a fulfilling life. Please remove any feelings of doubt, discontentment, and unhappiness. Fill my heart with joy. Thank you, God. Amen.

Questions for Thought or Discussion

1. How do I feel about being single?

2. What goals do I want to accomplish but am putting on hold until I get married?

3. What steps can I take today to begin reaching for my goals?

4. What activities do I need to eliminate, or whom in my life do I need to limit my time with, to take better care of myself?

CHAPTER 2

Moving Forward

❧ ◆ ❧

So, now you're divorced and you're wondering what's next. You're asking yourself, *What do I do now? Where do I begin to start over?* Before you make any major decisions, it's very important that you first put everything behind you. It's time to start thinking about how to move on with your life. Before you can do this, you have to let go of the relationship.

It's difficult to move forward physically if you're constantly looking back. Just think about it—you can't walk very fast and very far if you're looking behind while you walk or if you're walking backwards. Not only that, but it's also very possible to trip over something or run into something or somebody if you're looking back while you walk. The same theory applies in your personal life. You won't be able to move on with your life if you're constantly thinking about your past relationship.

You won't be able to concentrate or focus on your future. God has so many great things in store for you if you will look forward and stop looking back. Jeremiah 29:11 says, "For I know the plans I have for you, declares the LORD, plans to prosper you and not to harm you, plans to give you hope and a future." There are so many things in store for you, and you won't be able to see them if you're looking at and dwelling in the past. The apostle Paul knew that in order to move forward in life, we must forget those things that are behind: "Brothers, I do not consider myself yet to have taken hold of it. But one thing I do: Forgetting what is behind and straining toward what is ahead." (Philippians 3:13)

Sometimes thoughts of your past relationship can overcome you. It seems as if you just can't stop thinking about that person. An hour doesn't pass by without you thinking about him or her. You think about how things used to be. You think about the things he did for you that no one else did. You think about how she was different from all the other women. In a way, you don't want to move on and forget about the past. You keep thinking, *What if it's meant for us to be together? Maybe something will happen to make it all work out somehow. Maybe he'll change. Maybe she'll change her mind and ask me to come back.*

Once you have decided to let the relationship go and you feel confident about the decision, let it go and move on! Once you are convinced that moving on is the best thing to do, you must not look back. Forgetting is a healing process. If you're having trouble forgetting about the relationship, say a prayer and ask God to heal your mind of the memories. Ask God to remove the pain you have in your heart when you think of the person.

Certain places you visit or people you see may trigger that pain. For example, my husband and I had quite a few friends whom we visited often. After the divorce, whenever I met these friends, my heart would ache. I couldn't figure out why. I didn't have any ill feelings towards them. They hadn't done anything to hurt me. They were nice to me and I was nice to them. The encounters with them were very cordial, but for some reason I felt hurt inside when I saw them.

Finally, one day, I realized what was happening with me. Seeing them reminded me of something painful—my failed marriage. Seeing them made me feel hopeless. They had nothing whatsoever to do with the marriage breaking up, but seeing them reminded me of that experience, and this is what brought on the stabbing pain. The same thing would happen when I visited certain places. Certain restaurants, buildings, or parts of town I would go to would bring a pain in my chest. The pain was there because I was associating these places (subconsciously) with a painful experience. I had to ask God to heal me of the pain. I could not do it on my own. God had to do it. My heart needed healing. I simply prayed for God to take the pain, as if it were a physical bruise.

As you move on with your life, God will replace the pain with peace and confidence. You may have to temporarily (or even permanently) remove yourself from places that ignite memories and pain or where you know you'll meet people who remind you of the relationship. I had to do this. I had to stop visiting some of the places that my ex-husband and I used to visit. I took a different route instead of passing the same places we used to drive by. If you just can't bear the pain, it may be wise to do this for a while until your healing takes place. If certain places or people remind you of that person, consider making changes in these areas until the healing is complete.

Of course, forgetting the past takes time, as does healing any wound. With time, your physical body naturally heals itself when it's wounded. If you scrape your elbow and cause a serious bruise, the skin grows back over the scrape eventually, but it takes time. It takes even longer for it to heal if you bump into things during the healing process. It's the same with the ending of a relationship.

You must give yourself time to heal. While you're healing, you must take care of yourself and be careful not to "bump against" anything. This means keeping yourself from people and places that remind you of this painful experience, until you're ready and completely healed.

It also means keeping yourself from people who constantly talk negatively about your situation. If there are those in your past who insists on dwelling on your past, you must get away from these "toxic" people. Toxic people are people whose conversation and/or lifestyle are poisonous and detrimental to your growth. People who constantly talk negatively and say degrading things about you or your situation are toxic people. People who constantly bring up things in your past are toxic people. People who always complain about everything and anything are toxic people. You don't need these people in your life. You need people in your life who will support you as you move on toward the future. You need people in your life who will help you to keep looking forward and not backwards. Lovingly remove yourself from anyone, any place, or any-thing that continues to "scrape" your bruise during your healing process.

One very important step in forgetting the past is to stay away from the person you were in a relationship with as much as possible. This person will "scrape" your bruise worse than anything or anyone ever could. Even if the relationship ended peacefully, it's still wise to cut the emotional attachment with your ex. You won't be able to heal completely if you continue to indulge in a relationship of any nature with your ex. Of course, you may have to have contact to conduct business or to make visitation arrangements when there are children involved, but to continue an emotional or physical interaction with your ex will only delay the healing process. If the final decision is to sever the relationship and to move on with your lives, you should not associate with that person. The more you associate with your ex, the harder it will be for you to move on without him or her. Remember, it's hard to move forward when you're looking back.

It's not uncommon for couples who are in the process of divorce, or even divorced already, to continue a sexual relationship. They feel it's safe to do this. They say things like, "Well, this *is* my spouse." "At least I'm not sleeping with someone else." "It's better than sleeping around."

What they don't realize is that continuing to sleep with an ex-spouse, actually slows down the healing process.

Once you've decided to sever the relationship, you must carry this out in all of your activities, including sex. The quicker you move on, the quicker your healing process will begin. Any extensive interaction with this person, especially emotionally or physically engaging activity, prolongs the healing process.

I talked to a lady once who told me she continued to sleep with her husband while they were in the process of a divorce. She thought she was playing it safe by sleeping with her husband instead of sleeping with someone new. Boy was she wrong. Twice she contracted a sexually transmitted disease from him. Even though he was the only one she was sleeping with, she wasn't the only one he was sleeping with. I've seen misunderstandings like this happen many times between men and women. It's not safe mentally or physically to continue to sleep with the person you are in the process of divorcing.

Forgetting your past is a must if you want to go on to the future. A healing process must take place. The healing process can only take place with God's help and by you completely letting go of the relationship and everything involved. Pray and ask for God's strength to help you move forward. You'll never know what God has in store for your future until you let go of the past and look forward. Move forward to God's plan for your life.

How to Move Forward

1. **Isolate yourself from your ex as much as possible**. Cut off interactions with your ex as much as you can without disrupting your lifestyle or routine. The sooner you do this, the easier it will be to get on with your life. Contact with your ex could stir up feelings you don't want to renew. Conversations with him or her could grow into arguments and cause words to be said that neither of you mean to say. If he seems to call you about non-business-related issues (e.g., just want to chat, want to visit for a little while, just called to say hello, etc.), don't answer the phone. Don't participate in casual phone conversations or visit with the person. Don't give any opportunity for having a casual fling with your ex. You cannot afford to spend any time emotionally or physically with your ex when you are trying to move on. This would be like scratching a bruise when it's almost healed.

   Find replacements for routines you had with your ex. Plan some activities to replace those times you spent together so you won't be tempted to go back. If there are children involved, arrange for the children to be picked up at a relative's house or school, or if your ex must come to your house, meet him or her at the door. Try to make the visits as cordial and pleasant as possible for the children. Limit conversations with the ex when they pick up the children, especially if the conversations tend to turn negative.

   If you tend to argue during every visitation period, you will make the children uncomfortable. Arrange business discussion during a time when the children are not around. Keep telephone calls short and to the point.

2. **Make up in your mind that you will not look back but look forward**. If the separation or divorce is final, finalize it in your mind and in your heart. When you're having thoughts of regret and hopelessness, remind yourself of why the relationship ended. Those reasons likely still exist, and that's exactly what you'll be going back into if you reconcile with your ex-spouse. If you reunite and end up separating again, you will only prolong your healing process.

   Promise yourself that you will not become involved with your ex-spouse. Make a commitment to look forward to what God has in store for you in the future. You have to confirm this in your mind and make this promise to yourself before you can act upon it.

There will probably be times when your ex will try you to see if she can come back into your life. If you have resolved within yourself that it is over and you know for a fact that it's best for you to move on, stick to your guns. Be true to the promise you have made to yourself.

3. **Temporarily (or permanently) remove yourself from associations with that person**. Ask God to remove pain from your heart. Until this healing takes place, temporarily (or permanently) remove yourself from those associations. Are there special places you used to go together that make you sad when you go there now? If possible, stay away from these places until you are healed. Are there things in your home that bring painful memories? Have a garage sale and get rid of these things and replace them with something new. Do whatever you can to replace painful memories with things that will give you a fresh start.

4. **Ask God for forgiveness for any ill feelings you have toward your ex**. Remember, you must forgive others if you want to be forgiven. "And when you stand praying, if you hold anything against anyone, forgive him, so that your Father in heaven may forgive you your sins." (Mark 11:25) We all have areas of faults and weaknesses. Consider your own faults as you work toward forgiveness. Pray for your ex-spouse. Ask God to help you forgive your ex and anybody else you have bad feelings toward. If you feel someone else played a part in your marriage breakup—yes, even if there was infidelity involved—pray for that person.

If you were the one who left the marriage, you still need to pray that God will help you forgive your ex for things he may have done. Ask God to forgive you for the cause you had in the divorce and to remove any feelings of guilt you may have.

Let God deal with those people who have done you wrong. He's the only one who can speak to their heart. Don't try to seek revenge on anyone. You are responsible for your own actions in spite of how you've been treated. Don't compromise your relationship with God by trying to get even with someone. "But I tell you: Love your enemies and pray for those who persecute you." (Matthew 5:44)

5. **Recognize that when people say hurtful things to you, their painful words may not be intentional**. Friends, family, or other people around you may say things regarding your situation that will hurt you and make you feel bad. They'll make remarks that sound like they're blaming you for your marriage breakup. These remarks could come from anyone. When people attack you verbally or say things to you or about you that hurt you, you must recognize this as an attack from Satan. It's not an intentional attack by the person who made the offensive comment.

   Satan's main job is to kill, steal, and destroy (John 10:10). He will do this in any way he sees possible. He sits back and plans how he will destroy you. So, when you are attacked by painful words, recognize them as an evil assignment of Satan against your life. Just reject it. Don't believe it. People often don't realize they are hurting your feelings.

6. **Make a list of the unhealthy behaviors in the relationship**. If your relationship was emotionally or physically unhealthy, list those things that were harmful to you (e.g., verbal abuse, physical abuse, cheating, withholding intimacy or affection for extended periods). Having a list like this will help you move forward. Reminding yourself of the painful past will provide motivation to desire a better life. When you find yourself longing for that relationship, the list will remind you of how unhealthy the relationship was. Fortunately, as time passes, you will begin to heal and may forget some of the harmful things that happened in the relationship. The list will come in handy during those times and will help you avoid returning to an unhealthy relationship.

Scriptures for Moving Forward

Philippians 3:13 Brothers, I do not consider myself yet to have taken hold of it. But one thing I do: Forgetting what is behind and straining toward what is ahead.

Proverbs3:5–6 Trust in the Lord with all your heart and lean not on your own understanding; in all your ways acknowledge him, and he will make your paths straight.

Luke 6:37 Do not judge, and you will not be judged. Do not condemn, and you will not be condemned. Forgive, and you will be forgiven.

Prayer for Moving Forward

Lord, I thank you that you know the beginning and end of my life. You know exactly where I've been and where I'm going. You already know what I'm going through. You know the circumstances of my life. Lord, I pray that you touch and heal my heart of the hurt and pain I have suffered during this situation. I pray that you give me the strength to move on with my life, so I can fulfill the purpose and plans you have for me. Help me look forward and not backward. Give me a new heart and a new mind. Let your spirit overwhelm me when my mind wanders back to things in the past. Restore the joy in my heart and spirit.

Lord, I pray that your will be done in my ex's life. I pray for divine forgiveness in my heart. Help me forgive everyone who played a part in this separation. Remove all resentment and anger from my heart. Lord, Jesus, I look forward to what lies ahead, because I know you are holding my hand and leading me to your will for my life. I pray that you help me to keep my focus on you and not on the past. Thank you, God, Amen.

Questions for Thought or Discussion

1. What changes do I need to make in my life to let go of the past?

2. What places do I visit that stir up painful memories?

3. What activities am I involved in with my ex that are making it hard for me to let go?

4. What things or behaviors occurred in the relationship that were unhealthy for me?

5. What are some things I've always wanted to accomplish that I now have the opportunity to attempt?

CHAPTER 3

Managing the Grief of Divorce

ॐ ◆ ॐ

Ending any relationship can be painful, regardless of the circumstances. This person with whom you've spent so much time and shared so much of yourself will no longer be in your life. This person who you've actually given your heart to is no longer there. This person whom you have joined with physically and spiritually is now broken off from your being. Even if it was a bad relationship, there will be emptiness where something once was. Even if you were the one who left, there may still be feelings of devastation because of the loss.

I've talked to many who have experienced the death of a loved one. I noticed during their bereavement that they used some of the same terms as those going through divorce. One statement I hear a lot is, "It feels like someone is literally reaching inside me and pulling my heart out." This statement perfectly describes how I felt when I divorced. I felt as if someone had pulled my heart out. I felt as if someone had a knife in my heart and was twisting it. Every so often, I would cry because of the pain I felt. I couldn't control the pain. The only thing I could do was cry. There were times when I'd be at work and my eyes would fill with tears. I was hurt, disappointed that what I had intended to last forever had ended.

Another thing I've heard people in bereavement say is, "At first I was in shock." I felt this also. The day the separation occurred, I remember thinking, *Oh, this is not real, it's not really happening.* I would wake up in the morning, and one of my first thoughts would be, *Oh my God, my husband is gone. I'm all alone.* I was in shock.

I've even heard some talk about how they went through a period of anger. They were angry at their loved one for leaving them, or they were angry at someone else whom they felt caused the death (doctor, hospital, drunk driver, driver who ran the red light). They were angry that their loved one was no longer around.

Divorce brings feelings of shock, pain, sadness, and anger. There are times during the divorce when you feel as if you can't go on. You feel you don't have a reason to go on. You hurt every minute of the day. The shock and the stabbing pain seem as if it will never go away.

Believe it when I say the "grieving" period does pass and you eventually feel you *can* go on with your life. Sure, you probably still miss your spouse. You may feel sad that he is no longer with you. You may have a hard time getting used to the fact that the one you loved is no longer there. However, the intensity of the pain you feel gets lighter as time goes by.

There may be moments when life is difficult for you. If you find you are not handling this period well, consider meeting with a counselor or talking to someone you trust to help you get through this period. Don't try to go through it alone. Talk to a close friend about your feelings. Take life a day at a time. Try not to worry about tomorrow and how you will go on. Live in each moment of each day and make the best of it. Ask God for strength every morning when you wake up. He is the only one who can give you the inner strength you need.

Bereavement counselors say that the quickest way to get over the initial pain of a loved one's death is to go back to your daily routine as quickly as possible. Do the same with divorce. If you were working before the loss, go back to work. If you were in school, go back to school. Don't allow the divorce to paralyze you and cause you to cut off your goals.

Yes, you must allow yourself time to move through the stages of grief, but at some point, you must take the steps necessary to move on for your wellbeing. Go ahead and grieve, cry, and express whatever you're feeling during the process. In time, you will gain the strength you need to manage your emotions and do what you need to do to move on with your life.

Don't allow the grief of divorce to overtake you. Try not to think too much about what you're experiencing. It's only natural to worry when you are suffering divorce, but don't allow worrying to inhibit your normal activities. When you find yourself thinking about it too much, turn your attention to something more pleasant. Force yourself to continue to accomplish your daily activities. As the old saying goes, time heals all wounds. Do the best you can to manage the grief until the pain eventually leaves.

How to Manage the Grief of Divorce

1. **Take a good look at how you're handling the divorce emotionally and determine if you're handling it successfully or not.** Questions to ask yourself to determine this are: Do I have trouble sleeping at night? Have my eating habits declined? Do I feel like isolating myself from everyone? Have I lost energy to do things I used to do? If your answer to these questions is yes, you are probably not handling the divorce very well emotionally. Talk to someone you trust or find an experienced counselor.

2. **Go back to your daily routine as soon as possible.** It will be hard physically and emotionally, but you have to go back to your routine. Going back to your daily routine will help keep your mind off your problems.

3. **Volunteer to serve at church or in a community program.** This will keep your mind occupied while you heal emotionally and will also give you a sense of accomplishment while you rebuild your life. The time it takes to heal won't seem quite as long when you are busy. The rewarding feeling of helping others will help you feel better.

4. **Whenever you feel the urge to, cry.** Let your emotions out. If you're in a public place and you feel the need to cry, move to a private area and release your emotions. If you're at home, cry out to God. Talk to God as if he is your father. Let him know how you feel and tell him you need his help to make it through this. Crying helps to purge the pain and the anger inside. You will feel better afterwards.

5. **Give praises to God daily, especially when you don't feel like it.** Thank God for the new plan he has for your life (even if you don't know what it is yet). As you praise God daily, the spirit of praise will eventually take away the feeling of heaviness.

Scriptures for the Grief of Divorce

Isaiah 61:1, 3 He has sent me to bind up the brokenhearted, to proclaim freedom for the captives and release from darkness for the prisoners, to proclaim the year of the Lord's favor and the day of vengeance of our God, to comfort all who mourn, and provide for those who grieve in Zion; to bestow on them a crown of beauty instead of ashes, the oil of gladness instead of mourning, and a garment of praise instead of a spirit of despair. They will be called oaks of righteousness, a planting of the Lord for the display of his splendor.

Hebrews 13:5 For He hath said, I will never leave thee, nor forsake thee. (KJV)

John 14:1 Do not let your hearts be troubled. Trust in God; trust also in me.

Isaiah 53:4 Surely He has borne our griefs, and carried our sorrows; yet we esteemed Him stricken, smitten by God, and afflicted. (KJV)

Prayer for the Grief of Divorce

Lord, I know you love me and you care about everything that goes on in my life. I praise you for always being there for me and for being my loving father with open arms, for me to run to when I am hurting. God, right now, I am hurting. My heart is full of pain. I know you see my heart and the pain there. I know you don't like to see your children hurt. I know your son, Jesus, bore our sorrows and grief and carried our sicknesses and pains.

Lord, I pray that you remove the pain and heal my heart. Take away the heaviness. Give me a garment of praise for this spirit of heaviness. Replace this sadness with joy. Give me peace. Give me strength to go on. God, I know you said in your word you would never leave or forsake me. I ask that you give me the strength to trust you while I wait for the manifestation of your healing. Thank you, Lord, for sending the Holy Spirit to comfort, counsel, help, intercede for, defend, and strengthen me. In Jesus' name I pray. Amen.

Questions for Thought or Discussion

1. What do I have to be thankful for even in the midst of what I'm experiencing right now?

2. What activities can I begin to participate in that will help me begin the healing process?

3. At any given time, things could be worse than they are, but because of God's mercy, you are still in existence. How has God extended his mercy toward you in your situation? Thank God for this as you move forward in your new life.

CHAPTER 4

Managing Anger and Unforgiveness

ॐ◆ॐ

Not every divorce is about betrayal, but if you feel you have been mistreated, let go of any anger or unforgiveness you may have toward your ex. According to the Bible, it's okay to be angry as long as you don't allow it to cause you to sin (Ephesians 4:26). In your anger, don't attempt to seek revenge. Be careful about the decisions you make and the actions you take when you are angry. If you do something to get back at your ex, you may regret it later.

You may be angry because you feel someone has done you wrong. You feel as if you don't deserve what's happened. You're probably saying to yourself, *He has a lot of nerve. She walks all over other people, takes advantage of people, and uses people. He does things to people and expect people to put up with it. It's not right! How could she do this to me?*

Maybe a close friend or someone you know played a part somehow in the divorce. I've talked to several people through the years whose spouses cheated with their close friend or someone they knew.

Remember that God loves that person just as much as he does you. He forgives him or her just as much as he forgives you. But before we can be forgiven, we must forgive. Yes, that person was wrong. No, you did not deserve to be treated that way, but God forgives those who repent. And that's between God and that person. You must make sure things are right between you and God.

I'm not saying to suppress your anger. You are free to be angry. If you were betrayed, you have a right to be upset. You entrusted your life and heart to this person. You were building a life with this person. Maybe promises and vows made to you were broken. You must forgive your ex. It may take time, but you must forgive. You can't harbor unforgiveness in your heart. Release your anger the safest way you know how without sinning—jogging, talking to a counselor or friend, playing tennis, crying, kickboxing, whatever—but don't harbor unforgiveness.

25

Get rid of the anger and let it go. Don't dwell on what happened. Don't relive it over and over again in your mind. Let it go! Focus on the positive. Focus on the future. It's over and you have a new beginning. Remember, you can't move forward if you're looking back, and if you're constantly thinking about how he did you wrong, that means you're looking back. Looking back will keep you from growing and moving forward.

Perhaps you were not the "victim" in the divorce but the one who betrayed your spouse. Maybe you were the one who mistreated the other person. Maybe you were the one who left the marriage because you were not happy. Maybe you were the one who gave up and walked away. If this is the case, ask God for forgiveness, forgive yourself and let go of any anger you are withholding. Let go of the disappointment by talking to God about what happened.

Remember, God created us and knows all about us. He knows what we're going to do before we even act upon it. While you are spending time feeling ashamed, God is waiting for you to talk to him about it. He is faithful and just to forgive us of our sins when we repent (1 John 1:9). Don't you dare continue to wallow in unforgiveness. This will cause you to fail to move forward to what God has for you in the future. Learn from the mistakes you made in the relationship. Ask God to make you a better person and to help you make better choices. Ask him to help you with feelings of condemnation and allow him to lead you and guide you to what he has in store for you. Let go of the past. Forgive yourself and others. Move past the anger and unforgiveness and grasp what God has for your future.

How to Manage Anger and Unforgiveness

1. **Realize that we've all made mistakes at one time or another.** If you were betrayed, remember that even though this person acted horribly in your eyes, we all make mistakes from time to time. In order to be forgiven by God for the wrong we have done, we have to forgive others for the wrong they do to us. "Do not judge, and you will not be judged. Do not condemn, and you will not be condemned. Forgive, and you will be forgiven" (Luke 6:37).

2. **Let God handle your life and everyone involved.** God is in complete control of your life. He's had a plan for you since the day you were born. He knows all about you. He also knows all about your spouse and everyone else involved in the divorce. Allow God to accomplish what he has planned for your life. Don't waste time harboring feelings of anger and unforgiveness. Let those feelings go and accept forgiveness in your heart toward your ex and everyone else involved. Remember how God forgives you when you do things that are not right. Pray and ask God to help you to have compassion and kindness in your heart toward your ex. Trust God that he will handle the situation and work everything together for your good. Anger will only cause you to become bitter with time. Just pray for your ex and ask God to remove all anger and unforgiveness and allow God to work in your life.

3. **Don't indulge in arguments with your ex.** Continuing to hold conversations and argue with your ex can only stir up more anger and resentment. If you indulge in conversation with your ex, she will say something to stir up anger in you, especially if there are unresolved issues. If you try to talk to your ex to try to make sense out of the issues, he may say some things that cause you to become angry. Limit conversations and arguments with your ex. Don't spend endless conversations trying to figure out what happened and what went wrong.

4. **Pray for strength when those feelings of anger or unforgiveness arise.** When you feel the anger rising in you, change the thoughts that are stirring up the anger and ask God to give you strength at that moment. Ask God to replace the feelings of anger with peace. Walk away from situations you feel you cannot handle until you feel you have the strength you need.

Scriptures for Managing Anger and Unforgiveness

Matthew 5:44 But I say unto you, love your enemies, bless them that curse you, do good to them that hate you, and pray for them which despitefully use you, and persecute you. (KJV)

Romans 12:16–18 Live in harmony with one another. Do not be proud but be willing to associate with people of low position. Do not be conceited. Do not repay anyone evil for evil. Be careful to do what is right in the eyes of everybody. If it is possible, as far as it depends on you, live at peace with everyone.

Ephesians 4:26, 27, 31, 32 In your anger do not sin: Do not let the sun go down while you are still angry, and do not give the devil a foothold. Get rid of all bitterness, rage and anger, brawling and slander, along with every form of malice. Be kind and compassionate to one another, forgiving each other, just as in Christ God forgave you.

Prayer for Managing Anger and Unforgiveness

Father, I thank you for making me stronger and more mature through this experience. I praise you for the patience and forbearance you will give me through this. I pray for your son or daughter, who I feel has mistreated me. I am deeply hurt by this person. I am angry. I have resentment toward her. I have hatred in my heart for her. Lord, I pray that you forgive me for this. Help me to realize that I must forgive in my heart before you can forgive me. Give me a forgiving heart, Lord. God, I pray for (his/her name). You know her better than I do because she is your child too.

God, I pray that you have mercy on my ex. I pray that you will touch his heart and strengthen him in weak areas. I pray that you will have your way in his life and that your perfect will shall be done in him and through him. Lord, prepare my ex and strengthen him for your service. Help us to live peaceably while we're together on this earth. I praise you for your anointing, which destroys every yoke of bondage. I receive emotional healing from any stronghold he may have on me. Help me to be kind and compassionate towards this person, oh Lord. Thank you, God. Amen.

Questions for Thought or Discussion

1. What things have I not forgiven my ex for? List these things and ask for God's help to forgive.

2. What are some things that God has forgiven me for, for which I am grateful?

3. What are some things I can do to begin the forgiving process?

CHAPTER 5

Managing Low Self-Esteem

ॐ◆ॐ

O ne of the first thoughts that comes to mind when a relationship ends is, "What did I do wrong?" As I was going through my divorce, a very close friend asked me, "What do you think you did to make him leave?" This question shot me right in the heart.

It's quite normal to have these questions when someone has rejected you. But remember, it takes two to make or break a marriage. You can work your hardest and do all you can, and things still don't work out sometimes. The other person has to want it just as much as you do.

Whatever the reason is for the breakup, you can't go on blaming yourself, especially if you know you did all you could. You might even wonder, *What if there was something I wasn't doing right. I should have done this, or I should have done that. It was probably this or it was probably that. Now, what am I going to do? Nobody else is going to want me.*

I knew a lady whose husband cheated on her habitually. What's sad is that she knew he was cheating on her but tolerated it. Once she told me about the time she found another woman's purse in her husband's car. She said she drove to the woman's house to return it, and while she was there she asked the woman why her purse was in her husband's car. The woman told her she had been seeing her husband for some time.

There were many other incidents of her husband's infidelity over the years. In the time that I knew her, her appearance slowly began to fade. Early on, she was a good-looking, well-dressed woman who always took good care of herself. Over the years, she began to look worn in her appearance. She worried a lot and fought with her husband a lot. Her husband's unfaithfulness seemed to affect her health and her attitude.

Since I felt close enough to her, I asked her one day, "Why do you put up with this type of abuse?"

She looked at me and said, "April, no one else is going to want me."

31

I was so shocked to hear this reply. Here was a beautiful, intelligent young lady with a wonderful personality submitting herself to an abusive relationship, simply because of her self-esteem. She didn't believe anyone else would want her. She chose to tolerate an abusive relationship in order to have a man in her life, rather than choosing to have a safer, healthier life without him.

Why did she feel she had to tolerate abuse? Why did she feel no one else would ever want her? We all want to be loved and we all want companionship, but to tolerate this type of abuse just to have a companion is not healthy. When you tolerate disrespect from an unfaithful spouse, you are sacrificing your self-worth. You are giving up yourself. You are disrespecting yourself as you allow that person to disrespect you by cheating on you.

If you truly love and respect yourself, you will accept nothing less from your spouse. Someone else's treatment of you should not determine your self-worth. "Love the Lord your God with all your heart and with all your soul and with all your mind. This is the first and greatest commandment. And the second is like it: Love your neighbor as yourself" (Matthew 22:37–39).

Psalm 139 talks about how God knows all about us. He knows when you sit and when you rise. He knows your thoughts. He's familiar with all your ways. He knows what you're going to say before you say it. It's so wonderful to know that God knows all about you and still loves you. Knowing this should help you feel good about yourself.

There is nothing wrong with loving yourself. There is a difference, though, between loving yourself and being haughty, conceited, or high-minded. That's not what I'm talking about. I'm not even talking about self-confidence. I'm talking about self-esteem, knowing who you are in Christ. Once you realize who you are in Jesus Christ, you will have all of the self-esteem you need.

Healthy self-esteem will produce self-respect, self-confidence, and motivation. Is it your fault your partner left? It doesn't matter whose fault it was. If you know in your heart that you have repented for whatever part you played in the cause of the divorce, then you can't wallow in self-pity and unforgiveness of yourself. Accept God's forgiveness and move on.

The divorce is final, over and done with. Move on. Don't walk in condemnation. Don't live in the past. Accept forgiveness and allow God to restore your life.

If it was your spouse's action that prompted the divorce, don't try to figure out why it happened. Don't blame yourself. At this point, you have to accept the fact that it's over and concentrate on what's in store for your future. Be aware of who you are in Christ. Ask God to allow his personality to show through your personality. Ask him to work on your personality to make you more like him. Regardless of what you've been like in the past, focus on God and what he wants to do in your life now. You are a child of God, which means you're a king's kid. You are fearfully and wonderfully made. God has great things in store for you. He wants to use you for his glory. Focus on God and the potential to which he will raise you up. Don't look down on yourself.

Manage your self-esteem by remembering who you are in Christ.

How to Increase Your Self-esteem

1. **Learn the following scripture, meditate on it, and believe it in your heart.** I praise you because I am fearfully and wonderfully made; your works are wonderful, I know that full well. (Psalms 139:14). Walk and talk as if you believe it.

2. **Don't listen to the negative things your ex says to you.** If your ex tries to blame you for the failure of the marriage, don't accept the blame. If your ex tries to tell you what you didn't do right or did wrong, don't listen. Remember, it takes two to make or break a marriage. You're both accountable for what has happened, but it's not productive to dwell on the reasons why. Don't allow your ex to feed your feelings of failure with negative words. Forgive him or her and forgive yourself. Pick yourself up and move on.

3. **Make a list of your positive characteristics and continue to build them.** Get to know yourself as an individual. Look closely at the personality that God has given you. There are tons of personality assessments available that can give you a good start for finding your strengths and personality style. One that is popular is the DiSC *Personality Profile*. There are even assessments that will help reveal what your spiritual gifts are. One popular one is *Personalizing My Faith* assessment. Do some research and find a good assessment that will help you get to know you. Ask your friends to help you write a list of your attributes. God has given each of us a unique personality. We have been placed on this earth to use our personality for his glory. There is a part of God in all of our personalities. Ask God to reveal himself more and more in your personality as you get to know yourself. You've been a husband or a wife until now. It's time to let your individual personality show.

4. **Set a challenging goal for yourself that you've always wanted to accomplish and pursue it.** Nothing makes you feel better about yourself than accomplishing something you've always wanted to do. This will build your self-esteem greatly. Maybe there's a different type of job you've always wanted. Redo your resume and go for it. Maybe you've always wanted a bachelor's degree or always wanted to go back to school for a master's degree. Go to school. My goal was to learn how to swim. I signed up for swimming lessons at the local YMCA and did it. It took three different instructors to teach me, but I finally learned to swim. This also gave me the nerves to go out and get a better job. I updated my resume and went out and got a better job. My self-esteem increased tremendously after those accomplishments!

5. **If you don't want to set a business goal, start a fun project or hobby.** You may choose to start playing tennis, golf, scrap-booking, crochet, photography, or painting. Take piano or guitar lessons. You could join a local book club or quilt-making club. Pick something that would be challenging and thus rewarding for you. Choose something you think would be fun for you to spend your time doing. Having a fun project gives you something to do on a regular basis and helps you occupy your time.

6. **Enhance your appearance.** Now is a great time to get a fresh new start with a fresh new look. If you can afford it, go and get a new haircut. Buy some new outfits that will spice up your current wardrobe. Get a new look, a new style. It's been proven that enhancing the way you dress helps you feel better about yourself. It can be a temporary esteem booster until you're at that level you want to be.

Scriptures for Managing Low Self-esteem

Romans 13:9 Love your neighbor as yourself.

Ephesians 2:10 For we are God's workmanship, created in Christ Jesus to do good works, which God prepared in advance for us to do.

Psalms 139:14 I praise you because I am fearfully and wonderfully made; your works are wonderful, I know that full well.

Prayer for Low Self-esteem

Right now, Lord, I don't feel too good about myself. Circumstances have caused me to feel down on myself. I don't feel worth much. I almost feel as if nobody loves me and nobody cares. I don't have very much going for myself. I don't know if I'll ever be loved the way I desire to be loved. I don't even know what I want to do with my life or what my gift or calling is, but, Lord, I know that you know. Father, I thank you that I am wonderfully made. I praise you that I would not even exist unless there was a plan for my life.

I thank you that no one else in this world can do what you created me to do. I thank you that every hair on my head is numbered by you and that you care about every aspect of my life. I praise you that I am your child and you love me for who I am. You know all about me and still love me, because you see my potential and what I can become. God, I pray that you strengthen my heart. I pray that you increase my confidence in you and in your word. I pray that you make me a mighty woman/man of God. Lord, most of all I pray that you show me what my gift/calling is. Lead me to the ministry that you have for me. Amen.

Questions for Thought or Discussion

1. What are my positive attributes (things I'm good at)?

2. What have other people complimented me for?

3. What are some things I like about myself?

4. How do my friends see me? What would they say are my strengths?

5. Who are some people I admire? What qualities do I admire in them? Which of these qualities do I possess?

CHAPTER 6

Losing Your Mind?

ঌ◆ঌ

T here were times when I had such a difficult time comprehending what was happening in my life that I felt as if I would lose my mind. Certain things just wouldn't register or make sense. Things weren't turning out the way I had planned or believed they would. What I was seeing physically and in reality was conflicting with what I had always believed. I just could not comprehend what I was suffering.

I had such a hard time dealing with the divorce. It was so heavy on my mind. Day by day, I would relive everything in my mind. I kept playing back arguments and hurtful things that were said. I kept trying to figure out how the breakup could be happening right before my eyes and I didn't even know it. I begin to feel like I was losing my mind.

This feeling happens to us because we dwell on certain thoughts we shouldn't for way too long. Destructive thoughts enter our mind and we allow ourselves to ponder them instead of releasing them.

Have you ever seen a homeless person on the street talking to himself? I've seen this several times, and every time, I noticed the person was rambling words about how someone hurt him or how he wanted to hurt someone. Some rambled words of disappointment, anger, and pain. Somewhere along the way, that person got stuck in his thoughts of anger and resentment.

Sometimes thoughts of loneliness, disappointment, or confusion may enter your mind and you can't seem to let them go. When you are having constant destructive thoughts, you have to get a grip and take yourself out of those thoughts. When you find yourself thinking too heavily about your situation, stop and change your thoughts immediately. Take a few minutes to say a quick prayer. Tell God that you need help.

There were times when I would be bombarded with disturbing thoughts at work. The thoughts would begin to weigh me down with worry. I would stop immediately and say a quiet prayer to God. I would simply say, "Lord, I need you now. Please help me."

If you get to a point where you feel you can't handle the mental pressures on your own, say a quick prayer and ask God to help you. If you feel you need to, talk to someone. Don't allow those thoughts to cause you to get stuck in that mode of thinking.

One way to conquer the feeling of losing your mind is to manage your thoughts. You can manage your thoughts so they flow in a more productive way. If you don't manage your thoughts, they will eventually affect your actions and reactions. Your thoughts affect your attitude and the way you feel, which in turn affect your behavior. You have to control your thoughts to make sure they don't cause you to act in a negative way. You have to control your thoughts so they don't take control of you.

The way to turn your negative thoughts into positive thoughts is to make a conscious effort to replace your negative thoughts with positive ones. It takes practice, but you can do it. The Bible instructs us to cast down imaginations, and every high thing that exalts itself against the knowledge of God, and bring into captivity every thought to the obedience of Christ (2 Corinthians 10:5 KJV). This is exactly what I mean by replacing negative thoughts with positive ones. When those negative thoughts come, think about good things, pure things. Turn your negative thoughts towards something good.

Let me give you an example. Let's say you're driving to work one morning and begin to have negative thoughts. Ladies, let's imagine you're thinking, *I can't believe my husband left me. Why couldn't he love me? What's wrong with me? I'll never find anyone else to love me now. No one will want me with all of these kids. I'm too old to meet anyone else. I'll be alone for the rest of my life.*

Gentlemen, let's imagine you're thinking, *I treated her like a queen. I gave her everything, and she still wasn't happy with me. What did I do wrong?*

And the negative thoughts keep coming and coming.

You have to recognize that you are allowing destructive thoughts to linger too long. You have to turn the negative thoughts around and not get stuck in them. You do that in your mind. Let's look at your drive into work again and practice changing the negative thoughts into positive ones:

Negative Thought	Positive Thought
"I can't believe my husband left me. Why couldn't he love me?"	"My marriage is over, but God works everything together for my good. I know He will turn this into something good for me in the long run."
"What's wrong with me?"	"God made me in His image and everything He made was good. I will allow God's personality and love to show through me more and more each day. God loves me just the way I am."
"I'll never find anyone else to love me now. No one will want me with all of these kids. I'm too old to meet anyone else. I'll be alone for the rest of my life."	"God has a plan for my life and I'm going to trust Him to see me through this. I trust that if His plan is for me to be remarried, it will happen. He knows what I need and He knows my desire and I trust Him because I know He will do what's best for me."
I treated her like a queen. I gave her everything and she still wasn't happy with me. What did I do wrong?"	"I know in my heart I did all I could to make her happy. God is the only one who can complete her happiness. He knows that I did my best in the marriage because He knows all about me."

As you can see, it takes a conscious effort to manage your thoughts and control where your mind is headed. Every time you catch yourself talking negatively in your mind, turn that negative talk into positive talk. The more you do it, the more it will begin to happen naturally. In this way you'll be able to control and manage your thoughts and protect yourself from losing your mind.

How to Manage Your Thoughts

1. **Surround yourself with positive people.** Make sure you surround yourself with people who have positive attitudes and who don't speak negatively all of the time. I'm not talking about people who live in a fantasy world and refuse to be realistic about life. I'm talking about people who choose to have a positive outlook on life, people who know how to walk and talk in faith and live in peace, people who have encouraging conversation.

2. **Feed your mind with positive things—prayer, Bible, television, books, etc.** Make sure you are spending time with God by reading the Bible and by praying regularly. What you feed yourself mentally is what you will think about and give out. Find a good book to read that will encourage your heart. Local Christian bookstores always have a top-seller list of books. Find an inspirational book that you can read to help you stay encouraged. Find some good radio stations and television programs with good Bible teaching and inspirational music. Keep your spirit built and encouraged with inspirational messages daily.

3. **Meditate on the scripture weekly.** Pick at least one scripture to meditate on all week. Memorize that scripture and keep it on your mind and in your heart.

4. **Speak positive things.** There's a lot of power in what you speak. Sometimes speaking negatively about a situation makes it seem to get worse. Speak positive even when you don't feel good about it. If you can't find anything positive to say, just thank God for what he is going to do in your life in the future.

5. **Say a quick prayer when your thoughts are out of control.** Stop wherever you are and whisper a prayer to God. Just say, "Lord, I need you. Please help me." Do this whenever those thoughts get out of hand. This will help you to learn how to turn things over to God and allow him to manage them for you.

Scriptures for Managing Your Thoughts

Philippians 4:8 Finally, brothers, whatever is true, whatever is noble, whatever is right, whatever is pure, whatever is lovely, whatever is admirable—if anything is excellent or praiseworthy—think about such things.

Proverbs 16:3 Commit your works to the Lord and your thoughts will be established. (KJV)

Isaiah 26:3 Thou wilt keep him in perfect peace, whose mind is stayed on thee: because he trusteth in thee. (KJV)

Prayer for Managing Your Thoughts

Lord, I have been having some crazy thoughts. I feel like I am about to lose my mind. I can't seem to control my thoughts on my own. I need your help. Father, you said in your word that you would keep those in perfect peace whose mind is stayed on thee. I pray, Lord, that you will give me perfect peace. I need peace of mind. My mind is in turmoil right now as I try to figure out what is going on. Lord, I pray that you give me comfort and peace in you. Keep my mind. Direct my thoughts. Help me to keep my mind on you and not on my problems. I pray that you will help me to think good thoughts. Help me to think on those things that are pure, true, and holy. Thank you, dear Lord, for peace and strength. Amen.

Questions for Thought or Discussion

1. What activities do I participate in that feed my mind with positive things?

2. What activities do I need to eliminate that stir up negative emotions?

3. Which friends do I surround myself with who help motivate and encourage me?

4. What negative activities or friends do I need to limit my time with to avoid feeding any negative thoughts?

CHAPTER 7

Managing Loneliness

❧◆❧

There was a point in my life when I was so lonely I thought I would die. It was during my first year of college. I was living on campus. I had a close friend there, but she was busy with other things. I was very shy in high school and didn't grow out of it until my last year of college. As a result, during my first year I didn't have a lot of friends or do a lot of partying like some of the other college students did. I spent a lot of time alone in my dorm room feeling very lonely and sad. It was also a little scary being out on my own away from home. I attended school year-round every year, so I lived on campus during the summer also. In the summer, there weren't as many students on campus. I didn't know how I was going to make it through that time, but I did. It was very hard. The loneliness felt like a heavy blanket was covering me and weighing me down. It was heavy, and I couldn't shake it.

I experienced this type of loneliness again years later, after the divorce. At times, the loneliness was so heavy that I would just cry for hours. I felt as if no one cared. I felt so alone. I was even beginning to wonder if something was wrong with me, because I had serious mood swings where I would be happy one minute and sad and lonely the next. I just couldn't get rid of the lonely feeling. I would sit alone many nights hoping and praying that somebody, anybody, would call and talk to me. There were nights when I prayed for the phone to ring.

I was so lonely that even if I was at work or in a crowd of people, I would still feel lonely. I had a strong desire for companionship, or even just a friend to talk to, especially one of the opposite sex. I just couldn't seem to get rid of the heavy feeling. It made my heart ache. I would lie in bed at night praying for companionship, a friend. I would sit on the couch and try to think of someone to call to fill the void. There were nights when I had thoughts of going out to a nightclub or somewhere to find someone to spend time with.

Loneliness can be a dangerous thing if you don't control it. It can make you do things you wouldn't typically do. It can cause you to make decisions that you wouldn't make if you were thinking clearly. It can cause you to become desperate and do crazy things out of desperation.

Loneliness is something that visits most singles on a regular basis. I believe everyone desires to be loved and to give love. Some of us just want that special someone to spend our lives with. We want someone to spend time with, enjoy life with. We don't mind going to a movie or dinner alone, but sometimes we'd much rather have someone to go with. We want someone to talk to and share things with.

Loneliness is harder at sometimes than other times. During the holidays, you may feel even lonelier. On Valentine's Day, you may feel sad that you don't have someone to share that day with. As the flowers are being delivered in the office, you may wish it was you receiving them. Christmastime is very difficult, because this is a time when you're used to being with family, sharing fun traditions. There's a spirit in the air that just gives you the need to share the season with someone special. You want to hold hands with a special someone or cuddle under a warm fireplace.

The good news about loneliness is that it comes and goes. You'll have good days and bad days. Some days you'll be content and even happy about being single. Some days you'll be thankful for not having to deal with the work that relationships often require. You'll be glad, sometimes, that you can make decisions on your own or not have to discuss money with someone. There are other times, though, when you'll feel lonely. The loneliness comes and goes.

Something that has really helped me deal with loneliness is my trust in God. As I think about the thoughts I have during the moments of loneliness, I conclude that I'm feeling this way because at the moment I am not trusting God. Of course, it's natural to desire someone to be with. It's only natural to want to be loved. But God also knows exactly who you are and what you need. He knows what he's doing in your life. And for some reason, he has allowed you to be single at this point in your life. You have to trust him in that. You have to trust that if you're struggling with being single, he knows all about your struggle. God knows you better than you know yourself. He created you. God knows how difficult it is for you to be without someone, especially when you're used to being with someone on a regular basis. You have to trust that he knows what he's doing in your life. You have to trust him to comfort you and take care of you during the lonely times.

Trusting means you don't pick up the phone and call someone to replace that lonely feeling. Trusting means you don't go out and try to drink away the loneliness. Trusting means you don't have a "friend with benefits" that you call to take care of your needs. You have to trust God and be content with the fact that maybe he has someone for you or maybe he doesn't. When you rely on others to meet your needs immorally, you're not trusting God. You're taking matters into your own hands. God knows what's best for you. He knows how much you can handle.

Being involved in a singles ministry helps me tremendously with loneliness. The teaching and encouragement that I receive keeps me going. Most singles ministries are designed to teach singles how to live a victorious single life in Christ. A singles ministry is a great place to meet new people and make new friends. Through the years I've made many friends that I've shared many fun times with. I've learned so much about how to manage some of the more trying areas of single life. Being part of a singles ministry helps you in your endeavor to maintain a safe, healthy, and pure lifestyle, because you are receiving biblical teaching and support from others with whom you have something in common. With a good singles ministry, you'll have a good support group for the difficult times.

To manage loneliness, trust God for what he's doing in your life. Rest assured that he knows all about you and he loves you. He is there with you at all times, even during the lonely times.

How to Manage Loneliness

1. **Set up a routine schedule for activities you enjoy doing.** Schedule activities for certain nights of the week and make a routine of it. My schedule included something fun every Friday night. I called it "family night" for me and my daughter when she was very young. For some reason I tended to feel lonely more on Friday and Sunday nights than at any other time. Every Friday, I would schedule the movie time and theatre before I even left work so I would have something to look forward to, and then my daughter and I would go to see the movie. Sometimes we went to a dollar theatre to save money or we would rent a movie at the video store, but we always had a movie or something planned for Friday night. Other ideas for routine activities are exercising at the gym, joining a volunteer program, visiting the elderly at the nursing homes, visiting children in the terminal illness ward, and meeting with friends at a coffeehouse. You can meet many people and make new friends when you participate in various activities. There are so many things you can get involved in to make valuable use of your time and help you get through the times of loneliness. Before you know it, those times won't be as intense as they once were.

2. **Pray and meditate on God's word daily**. As you fill your heart, mind, and spirit with God's word, it will come to your aid during those times of loneliness. Reading God's word and really receiving it and believing it will give you something to call on during those trying times. When you feel loneliness coming on, think back on the scriptures you've read and ask God for strength in that moment. God's word will give you the strength you will need during those times.

3. **Make a list of fun things you like to do or people you like to visit.** Make a list of fun activities you like to participate in (e.g., jogging, knitting, sports, visiting friends, painting, dancing, playing video games, skating, swimming). When you feel lonely, grab your list and do something on it. Don't sit there and wallow in self-pity or loneliness. Take action immediately by doing something fun. Loneliness tends to weigh you down physically, so it will take a lot of effort to pull yourself up and do something, but do it anyway. You will feel a lot better if you get up immediately and do something to make yourself feel better.

4. **Get involved in a local singles group or organization for something you enjoy.** Most churches have a singles ministry. Most of them also allow singles to join the singles group, whether you're a member of that church or not. Find a local singles ministry that focuses on solid Bible teaching and uplifting fellowship with other singles. Get involved in the fun activities so that you can meet new people. As you get involved in the activities, you will gain friendships and associations with others and will be able to support each other and help each other enjoy single life. If you don't care to join a singles ministry, join an organization for something you enjoy doing— perhaps a book club, bowling league, volleyball team, or baseball team.

5. **Realize that the intensity of loneliness you're feeling right now is only temporary.** It may seem like forever, but the loneliness will eventually go away. Of course, at times you may feel alone and desire companionship—that's only natural. However, in time, the intensity of the loneliness you're feeling will decrease. You won't feel heavy, like you do now. Take these steps to press through the loneliness. Thank God now for the victory you will eventually see.

Scriptures for Managing Loneliness

Proverbs 18:24 A man of many companions may come to ruin, but there is a friend who sticks closer than a brother.

Isaiah 10:27 It shall come to pass in that day that his burden will be taken away from your shoulder, and his yoke from your neck, And the yoke will be destroyed because of the anointing. (KJV)

Hebrews 13:5 Let your conduct be without covetousness; be content with such things as you have. For he himself has said, "I will never leave you nor forsake you." (KJV)

Isaiah 41:10 So do not fear, for I am with you; do not be dismayed, for I am your God. I will strengthen you and help you; I will uphold you with my righteous right hand.

Prayer for Managing Loneliness

Father, you said in your word that you would never leave me or forsake me. I thank you for being with me every step of the way. I praise you for carrying me during these times of loneliness. Lord, I thank you for holding my hand even now. I am not alone. I pray Lord that you lift this spirit of loneliness away from me. I pray for joy and peace of mind. I pray that you feel my empty heart with gladness. Thank you, Lord, for being with me, leading me, and guiding me to that place you have for me. Lord, I ask that I may meet people who can help me during this difficult time. I pray for divine appointments with those you want to be in my life so that we can encourage one another. Lord, I thank you for being my friend; you are closer than a brother to me. Thank you for encouraging my heart and filling my heart with peace and gladness. Amen.

Questions for Thought or Discussion

1. Which days/times do I feel most lonely?

2. What activities have I planned to offset the times when I feel loneliest?

3. What local organization or single ministry will I visit this month to be able to give and receive support for the lonely times?

4. How can I show God that I trust him when I am feeling lonely?

CHAPTER 8

Single Parenting

❧ ◆ ❦

Children imitate what they see adults do. Parents send a message to their children with everything they do and say. And believe me, children watch both. Because of this, you have to watch what you say and do around your children. You want to set a good example for them and show them how to behave in the face of adversity. You should train your children in the word of God and teach them the difference between right and wrong so they'll know the difference when they are older.

Children need to know how to make righteous decisions. They need to know the difference between holy and unholy, righteousness and unrighteousness. How will they know how to make righteous decisions if they don't know the difference between right and wrong? I've heard people say, "Well I raised my child in church, and he still turned out bad." You cannot control what your children will become. You can only do your best to teach them. You have to give all you can to teach them how to live righteously and then trust God to help them when they move out on their own.

Maybe you have joint custody of your children. Perhaps you see them every other weekend or on holidays, or you have some other type of arrangement. It's even more critical during these times that you share Christ with them as much as you can. Loving them is the best way to share Christ with them. If you spend the entire time preaching to them or giving them advice, you may come across as a fussy parent. I spoke with someone who was sad that his teenage daughter no longer wanted to visit him. He had joint custody and the arrangement was for her to spend every weekend with him, but she no longer wanted to visit him. I asked him what their visits were usually like. He said he tried to use their time together to correct her bad habits and to tell her what she needed to do in the future. He said they were even beginning to argue a lot during recent visits. He said she told him in their last visit that he was always trying to tell her what to do.

Don't try to make up for time you don't get to spend with your children by forcing a lot of discipline and advice into your visits. Pray and ask God to bless the limited time you have together. As you trust God with your visits, the teaching, advice, and discipline will lovingly flow. Your children will be more receptive of your teaching, because they will see your love and will see God working in you.

The best way to show the love of Christ is through your loving and gentle actions. Let them see how God works in your life. Even though the time you have with them may seem short, you can still make it valuable by loving them and allowing God to control your visits. Knowing that God is in control of your parenting and that you are doing all you can to be a good parent will encourage you during those times when you feel sad about not having enough time with them.

Regular attendance in a solid Bible-teaching church is critical in successful single parenting. Some churches have strong youth programs that teach the Bible on a level that children can understand and apply to their lives. Try to find a church that provides what you and your children need to help you grow and mature spiritually.

In addition to attending church regularly, make sure you teach them and show them how to trust God at home. Pray with them regularly. Teach them how to pray for themselves and others. Do this by praying for them when they are sick and showing them how to pray for themselves. When someone asks you to pray for them, pray for them with your children. Let your children know the prayer request before you pray. This will help your children see how God answers prayers and will build their faith and trust in God.

Read the Bible with them and make sure they understood it and know how to apply it to their lives. When they have questions or problems, show them how to find answers and help in the word of God. Feed them with Godly entertainment and don't let them watch every program they want to watch on television. Sometimes in joint custody situations, you may tend to be more lenient during your scheduled visits because you don't want to look like "the bad parent." Regardless of the limited time you have with your children, you must always be a good example for them. It's your responsibility as their parent to monitor everything they have access to, because whatever they watch will feed their minds and hearts.

The best way to teach your kids how to trust God is to live a life that shows them that you trust God. When you have difficult times, pray about them with your children so they can watch how God answers prayers.

When someone you know is sick or in trouble, pray for them with your children so they can see how God helps and heals. They should see you praying. They should see you reading the Bible. If possible, have a regular time of Bible reading and prayer with your children. You can do something as simple as reading one chapter each night or each week. I can't remember one night when I did not see my mom on her knees praying at nighttime before she went to bed. And there were many times I woke up to find her checking on me at night as I slept. This showed me her love for God and her love for me. What a valuable lesson! Show your children the love of God by loving them and loving God with them.

Show your children how you manage other areas of your life, such as money, friendships, and hardship. Show them how to maintain discipline in these areas by practicing self-control. Of course, you won't always have self-control, but you should show your children that even though you are not perfect, God is there to help you get back on track whenever you mess up. Show them that they need God in their lives to help manage life. Show them how God is your source for everything and that you can't make it without God.

Spend as much quality time as you can with your children, especially when you have joint custody and limited time. Show them you love them by dedicating your time to them and not sending them to a babysitter. Quality time does not have to involve spending money. You could watch a movie together at home, play board games, ride bikes, or go for a walk. Nothing says, "I love you" more to children than spending time with them. Make sure you have a regularly scheduled time for just you and your children.

Work is obviously important. Friendships and socializing are critical as you go through life. Children, however, are your most important priority when you are single. Your children's happiness and wellbeing should come before anything else going on in your life. God has entrusted you with their heart, mind, and spirit. Do your part to make sure they are safe and secure. Love them and take care of them the best way you can. Pray and ask God to help you be the parent you should be for them.

How to Manage Single Parenting

1. **Spend quality time with your children to let them know you love them and that they are important.** The most precious time in my life is the time I spend with my daughter on a regular basis. I enjoy spending time with her more than any time I spend with my friends. When my daughter became a teenager, one of my favorite things we would do is what we called "Triple S" (shopping, show, and sushi). Almost every Saturday, we would get up, eat a big breakfast, and do household chores. Then we would go out for shopping and a movie and then finish the day by going to eat sushi. We also occasionally have karaoke night, when we take turns singing on our karaoke machine at home. We even have nights on the weekend where we pull a mattress into the theater room, eat snacks, and watch movies all night. Spending quality time with your children is very important, and it means so much to them. Quality time could involve reading a book together, playing catch or basketball, going to the library, having lunch with them at school, watching a movie together, playing cards, singing songs, building a tent, playing a board game, going to a theatre, or going to the park. Nothing tells your children you love them like spending time with them. If you have a busy schedule, designate special time each week with your child. Let them know they are special to you by spending time with them and listening to them.

2. **Tell them you love them constantly.** Sometimes children of divorced parents feel as if the divorce is their fault somehow. They blame the whole thing on something they may have done. They wonder why the absent parent left them. They wonder how someone could love them and still leave. Give them confidence and security by telling them how much you love them. Let them know it was not their fault. Let them know you love them in spite of the situation. Show them love and affection through your words.

3. **Take the time to answer their questions. Don't ignore them.** Children have many questions when parents are divorcing. There is a lot they don't understand. When they ask questions, they are really just trying to understand what went wrong and if it was their fault. They also wonder if it's possible their parents could reunite. Don't brush them off when they ask questions. Remember, a child's number one need (along with your love, of course) is security. As you answer their questions, keep this in mind: regardless of the questions they ask,

they are really looking for security. Give them a reasonable answer without getting into too much detail. Try to answer their questions while remembering their main concern. For example, they may ask, "Did Dad do something wrong?" or "Did Mom not like living with us?" or "Did I do something to make Dad leave?" Remember, the reasoning behind their questions is the need for security. So, in your answer, make sure you help them feel secure. You could say something like, "Baby, Mom and Dad are trying to work some things out right now. Everything will be fine. Remember we both love you no matter what."

Take the time to answer their questions or just let them talk about how they are feeling. Don't ignore them. Show them you love them by listening.

4. **Don't talk negatively about the absent parent.** Your child is a part of your spouse, so if you talk negatively about your ex, you will make your child feel bad. This is a person I'm sure they love, so don't hurt them by talking badly about that person. Try to limit conversations about your ex with your children, especially if the conversations turn negative. Remember, this person is your child's mom or dad. Your children still love him/her. Don't try to create any negative emotions in your children towards your ex. Trying to stir up negative feelings in your child toward your ex only makes things harder for your child.

5. **Don't introduce new companions to your child too quickly after the divorce.** Remember, security is a child's number one need. Introducing companions to your child too quickly sends signals of instability. They won't feel very secure knowing Mommy or Daddy just left and having to adjust to somebody new. Give the child time to heal emotionally from the divorce. Spend some time with your children helping them to deal with everything before you decide to introduce them to someone else.

6. **Show your child how to honor God and be an example of righteousness.** Being a parent is an honorable and trustworthy responsibility. God has trusted you enough to bless you with a child. Being able to physically produce a child is a miracle in itself. God has blessed you with this miracle and trusts you to be an example of his love with your children. Your responsibility as your child's parent is to honor God in all that you say and do. Show your children how to live righteously in your behavior and how to live holy in how you treat others.

Show them how to make righteous decisions. Use this very difficult time and any other trying time to show your children how to pray, and trust God for guidance. Be careful about what you do and say in front of them. Live righteously before them. Don't let "companions" sleep over in your home. Don't allow ungodly activity in your home. Show them how to honor God in your daily activities. Show them the love of God. What a wonderful opportunity—to raise Godly children in a negative world. You can do this if you live a Godly life of prayer, read God's word with them, and show them how to apply the word of God. Share God with them day and night.

Scriptures for Single Parenting

Deuteronomy 6:6–7 These commandments that I give you today are to be upon your hearts. Impress them on your children. Talk about them when you sit at home and when you walk along the road, when you lie down and when you get up.

Ephesians 6:4 And, ye fathers, provoke not your children to wrath: but bring them up in the nurture and admonition of the Lord. (KJV)

Prayer for Single Parenting

Lord, I thank you so much for entrusting me with my children. Children are very dear to you, and I thank you for entrusting me with something as precious as their lives. God, I pray that you will give me wisdom and guidance as I raise my children to be like you. I pray that your divine love will shine through me and touch their hearts. I pray that you will give me the strength and courage I need to be an example of your love and holiness to my children. Anoint me to speak your word in truth and love to them day in and day out. Amen.

Questions for Thought or Discussion

1. How often do I spend quality time with my children (once or twice a week, three times a week or more)?

2. How many times a day do I tell my children I love them?

3. What activities do I participate in that show my children the love of God?

4. What day of the week can I spend at least fifteen minutes sharing the word of God with my children?

CHAPTER 9

Managing Your Money

❧ ◆ ❦

As soon as you realize you are now going to have to manage your finances without a spouse, call a financial expert or accountant to help. If you prefer not to see a financial expert, start managing your finances by creating a simple budget. There are many books that can show you how to create a budget. Before you do a budget, take a quick look at your financial situation:

1. Get a sheet of paper.

2. Draw a vertical line down the middle of the paper and make two lists, side by side. (You could use Microsoft Excel to make your list also.)

3. The first list should include a list of your income. The second list should include a list of your expenses.

4. Add the totals for each list. How do they match up? Are you ahead or behind? Do your expenses exceed your income?

5. If your expenses do exceed your income, look at your list of expenses and put a star next to the ones that are optional or that can be reduced. How much can they be reduced? Is there any way you can eliminate or reduce expenses that are not starred?

Now, you are ready to create a budget. By creating a budget, you will know if you have enough income to maintain your lifestyle or if you need to earn more. Some people think a budget means keeping a record of the money you spend after you have spent it. In contrast, a budget is assigning an estimated amount for a particular purpose *before* you spend it.

The only way you will be able to manage your money efficiently is by forecasting an estimate of how much you will spend. Assigning an estimated amount for everything lets you know in advance how much you should spend so you won't overspend. It helps you to keep your spending limits within your income level.

You can create a budget using a Microsoft Excel spreadsheet. You can also use a software application to help you manage your personal finance. Some examples of some of the software programs you can use for budgeting and personal finance are Microsoft Money, Intuit Quicken, and Moneydance. To be able to generate a true forecast for how much you will spend, your budget should include all your sources of income (salary, child support, bonuses, etc.) and all your expenses (utilities, credit cards, mortgage/rent, car payment, gym, groceries, gas, savings, gifts, medical bills, dry cleaning, grooming, etc.). If you have children and are the non-custodial parent, consider adding child support to your list of expenses and begin paying right away, even if you haven't received a court order to do so. Your children will need the financial support. This will also help you avoid having to pay back support later.

Below is a sample of a monthly budget. You may have more items to put in your list of expenses, but the example gives you an idea of how to design your budget.

	January	February	March	April
Tithe/offering	400	400	400	400
Mortgage	1200	1200	1200	1200
Car payment	400	400	400	400
Car insurance	100	100	100	100
Gas	120	120	120	120
Cable	100	100	100	100
Groceries	300	300	300	300
Electric	200	200	200	200
Water	65	65	65	65
Phone	80	80	80	80
Cell phone	80	80	80	80
Credit card 1	150	150	150	150
Credit card 2	80	80	80	80
Savings	100	100	100	100
Gifts/shopping	200	200	200	200
Entertainment	200	200	200	200
Total bills	**3775**	**3775**	**3775**	**3775**
Total income	**4000**	**4000**	**4000**	**4000**
Left over	**225**	**225**	**225**	**225**

You'll notice I included entertainment, shopping, and even gas in the budget. It's important that you include every area where you spend money so you'll have an accurate account of where your money will go. The credit card payments should be more than the minimum payment amount to pay toward your accrued debt. Also, itemize your income if you receive income from more than one source. (Example: Child support, alimony, retirement) Be sure to create a budget *before* you get paid.

The previous example shows a budget for monthly pay, but if you're paid bi-weekly, create a budget for each pay period. To do this, split each month into two two-week columns. Then pay your bills that are due early in the month with your first paycheck and the bills due later in the month with your second paycheck. Split your mortgage or rent payments into two payments so you won't have to spend too much at one time. Do this by saving half the rent or mortgage payment with one paycheck and then pay your rent or mortgage when you get the other half the next paycheck. See the example below.

	Jan 1	Jan 15	Feb 1	Feb 15
Tithe/offering	200	200	200	200
Rent/mortgage	600	600	600	600
Car payment		400		400
Car insurance	100		100	
Gas	60	60	60	60
Cable	100		100	
Groceries	150	150	150	150
Electric	200		200	
Water		65		65
Phone	80		80	
Cell phone		80		80
Credit card 1	150		150	
Credit card 2		80		80
Savings	50	50	50	50
Gifts/shopping	100	100	100	100
Entertainment	100	100	100	100
Total bills	**1890**	**1885**	**1890**	**1885**
Total income	**2000**	**2000**	**2000**	**2000**
Left over	**110**	**115**	**110**	**115**

Make sure to include money for entertainment, such as movies and dinner. Try to stay within the budget for each item. Creating a budget helps you to save money for things you want to accomplish later. It can also help limit the money spent on credit cards. Managing a budget is important as you work to rebuild cash flow and financial security.

Whatever you do, try not to put more debt on your credit card. Adding debt to your credit cards will ultimately lead you into a financial dilemma. Instead of adding debt to your credit cards, it's better to cut back on unnecessary expenses or increase your income.

After you have created a budget, you may find that your mortgage or rent is too high for the income you have. If so, one thing to consider is selling the house or looking for a less expensive place to rent. Before you decide to sell your house, be sure to speak with a financial expert. Remember, your house is an asset as well as a home. The interest on your house is a huge tax benefit. If you have children, you have to consider their emotional needs also. If you received the house through a divorce settlement or judge's decree, think carefully about whether you have enough cash to live comfortably in the house or whether you should move into a less expensive place. If the monthly payments on the house are small and you can afford them, consider staying where you are.

You may determine you need to earn more income. You may decide you need a better paying job, or you may need to get a part-time job for a while. Before you start looking for a job, make sure you're headed for a job you would enjoy doing. When you do work you enjoy, it doesn't really feel like work. Before you start your job search, make a list of things you're interested in (e.g., typing, computer work, cooking, planning, child care, government, retail). Then, if possible, look for work in these areas.

Local colleges offer adult education courses where you can increase your skills and credentials. When I divorced, I had a job with a decent income, but after looking at my expenses, I realized I needed more money to pay the bills. I found some free computer courses at a local community center and completed the courses in months. I was able to add these computer skills to my resume, making myself more marketable and worth more money. I also talked to my manager at work about what I needed to do to receive a promotion. I worked hard to get promoted and increased my income.

If you were a non-income spouse, gaining employment will give you the ability to enroll in a retirement program, and you may even be able to purchase company stock. If you haven't worked for a number of years, getting back into the workforce will take some time getting used to, but it can ultimately reward you with more than just financial security. You will eventually begin to feel self-sufficient. You will meet new people. And you might even find that going into the workforce again takes your mind off of the problems related to your divorce.

One of the most common problems that comes up because of divorce is negative impact on personal credit. Good credit is vital. If you have been working during the marriage, your credit rating will not be affected by your divorce unless you and your spouse had joint accounts and failed to pay those bills on time, or if you stopped paying them after you separated. Be aware that the accounts you held with your spouse will show in your credit report. There's really not a lot you can do about that.

If you and your spouse had joint debts (taxes filed jointly, mortgage, car loans, credit cards) and you were the non-income spouse, you might have your name on the mortgage or car loan statement anyway; this means you are in debt—even though you have no income to offset the debt.

Creditors don't care if you are divorced when you owe them. The only thing they care about is how they will get their money back. They are not bound by the divorce settlement. They will hold both people liable for payment, even a non-income spouse. As far as the credit card companies are concerned, you remain responsible for all the joint credit card debt your spouse incurs.

The best thing for you to do is to get a copy of your credit report to see exactly what's listed. You can dispute any records in your report for which you were not joint account holder. Keep your divorce decree handy to show creditors the accounts you were released from in the divorce. Some creditors will take this into account when you apply for new credit. Eventually you will be able to create or reestablish your own personal credit history.

The sooner you assess your financial situation and come to terms with your true financial means, the sooner you will be able to take care of yourself.

One of the questions that frequently come up among single people who attend church is, "Do I have to tithe?" Times can get hard financially as you go through the whole divorce process. Often divorce results in financial suffering and great loss. During these times, it may become difficult to make tithe and offering a priority.

It's times like this that we ask, "Is tithing really necessary?" Through the years I've met so many people, single and married, who have asked the question, "Isn't tithing part of an Old Testament law that we no longer have to follow?" I asked myself that question for a long time. I wondered if tithing is really a part of the Christian life. Well, one day that question was answered for me. I read something in the New Testament that I didn't even know was there. I was surprised to find New Testament scriptures about tithing. When I read it, I realized that tithing is not just an Old Testament law. In Matthew 23:23, Jesus said, "Woe to you, teachers of the law and Pharisees, you hypocrites! You give a tenth of your spices— mint, dill and cumin. But you have neglected the more important matters of the law—justice, mercy and faithfulness. You should have practiced the latter, without neglecting the former." You can see in this scripture that Jesus believes tithing should not be neglected. This was very enlightening for me.

When I was married, I gave tithe faithfully. I didn't give it a second thought. But during the separation and after the divorce, things were really hard for me financially. I had a lot of financial debt that I was paying with a single income. I barely had any money left after I paid bills each pay period. I felt I just couldn't afford to give tithe, so I didn't. I did, however, give a "special offering." My special offering was a sacrificial amount that I was able to fit into my budget. I did this for months. I felt good about myself for giving my special offering. I believed that God would understand and bless my special offering.

Then, one day, I was visiting my mom and was talking to her about my bills. That's when she asked me a question that really made me think.

"April, are you paying your tithe?" she asked.

"Well, I give a certain amount in the offering each time," I replied. "Is it ten percent of your income?" she inquired.

"No," I said.

"Well, that's not your tithe then," she informed.

When she said that, her words really made me stop and think.

Weeks later, as I was sitting in church one Sunday, the minister read a scripture that made me stop and think about tithing again. He read a very familiar passage that I've heard so many times before, but this time there were a couple of words that really stood out for me. He read Malachi 3:8–10. The tenth verse reads, "Bring ye all the tithes into the storehouse, that there may be meat in mine house, and prove me now herewith, saith the LORD of hosts, if I will not open you the windows of heaven, and pour you out a blessing, that there shall not be room enough to receive it" (KJV). The words that stood out were "prove me now herewith." It was as if God himself was saying to me, "April, give it a try. Try me. Try me and see if I don't bless you bountifully." These words were spoken to me so softly but so strongly. I felt a strong urge to commit at that moment to give tithe.

So, I committed in my heart—and to God—to faithfully give tithe. I committed to giving tithe regardless of any financial challenges I would encounter. That day after church service ended, I went home and pulled out my budget spreadsheet and added tithe to the top of my budget to show that tithe would be priority.

It's amazing what began to happen in my life. As I begin to worship God in giving tithe and offering, I began to experience joy and fulfillment in my life like never before. Such contentment and peace came into my life. Not only that, but I received many financial blessings that I know came directly from God. That same year, I closed on a brand-new home. I was able to purchase the house with no closing costs, no money down, and a very low interest rate. The house was an answer to prayer for me. I heard about people being able to move into a brand-new house with no money and I prayed for that for myself. It was so amazing when God did that for me.

That same year, I received another financial blessing in the form of a bonus check at work. This was an unexpected bonus because of the financial state the company was in at the time. Receiving the bonus during a time like this only proved to me what God can do when I trust him. It was as if God was standing there looking at me saying, "See, just try me and trust me and see what I can do for you."

Since then, there have been so many other financial blessings in my life. Years before, I would hear people in church testifying about checks they received in the mail unexpectedly. That was so amazing to me. I have to admit that I sometimes wondered if this was really happening. I often wondered where those checks were coming from. I prayed that it would happen to me, but it never did.

Well, the same year I begin to tithe faithfully, I received checks in the mail that I did not expect. It was so amazing. I thought to myself, "Wow, this really happens." It was so exciting! I received a check from my mortgage company, a nice tax refund, and an appreciation check from my utility company for not switching. Giving tithe and offering has been such a blessing to me spiritually and financially. The greatest blessing is that all my needs are always met. No matter what my bills and income look like each month, I always have more than enough. Even when unexpected expenses arise, God always provides the income to pay for them. God provides for me over and over again.

I am not saying here that the only way you will be blessed is by giving tithe. I'm saying God loves a cheerful giver, and you should give according to what you have purposed in your heart and give cheerfully (2 Corinthians 9:7). Whatever the amount is that you choose to give, as long as you put God first in giving and in every other part of your life, you are sure to reach your single fullest potential. Giving your money, time, services, and especially love to others shows God that you love and trust him in every aspect of your life.

How to Manage Your Money

1. **Dedicate your income and your financial decisions to God by worshipping him in your giving.** You do this by cheerfully and freely setting aside an amount that you will give to the church or ministry where you are receiving biblical teaching. Ask God how much you should give. Purpose in your heart to honor God by putting him first in your giving. Make your offering a priority over other financial commitments. As you give, ask God to show you how to make wise financial decisions.

2. **Sincerely worship God through your giving.** Give honor and worship to God by giving to the ministry of your choice. If you don't have an income, give your time, prayer, and support to others in need. When you don't have an income from which to tithe, you can tithe by giving your time to God's service in helping others or volunteering at church. More than anything, give your love to others as much as possible.

3. **Create a monthly budget of all your expenses and income with your tithe or offering at the top of the list and stick to your budget as much as possible.** Create a budget to help manage your income and expenses. You will have more control over spending with a budget. Make sure to include an amount for fun activities.

4. **Eliminate any spending habits that are not necessary.** Look at your budget and try to cut unnecessary expenses. Expanded cable, advanced cell phone capabilities, and excessive shopping are possible items you can cut. The sacrifice you make here will help you to save money in the long term.

5. **Create an emergency account with at least $1,500 so you won't have to use credit for emergency situations.** Save as much as you can each pay period for emergencies. You never know when emergencies will occur. That's why they're called emergencies. Having money in an account for car repairs, travel, and other unexpected expenses will prevent you from having to use your credit cards.

   Don't worry about saving a large amount each paycheck. Whatever you save will accumulate.

6. **Try to save money whenever possible.** Try to save money or cut costs whenever possible. Here are some money-saving tips:

   - Eat out only on the weekends or maybe one or two days of the week. Buy groceries and cook at home. You'll spend approximately 30 percent more eating out than cooking dinner and eating at home.

   - Find out the daily specials for local restaurants and visit on those days. For example, some restaurants allow children to eat free on certain nights of the week. Also, there are restaurants where you can get two meals for the price of one on certain nights.

   - Check out movies from the public library instead of the local video store. Library videos are free and there is usually a decent selection.

   - Clip coupons and use them. Be careful that you're not clipping coupons for items you don't normally buy.

   - If you have credit cards, check into consolidating all of them to one credit card with a lower interest rate. Keep one major credit card for emergency purchases or travel.

   - Go to theatres that charge discount prices for movies that are a little older instead of paying full charge for movies with new releases.

   - Take your less expensive clothes to a discount cleaner. Wash your "wash and wear" clothes at home using the cycle for delicate fabrics.

Scriptures for Managing Your Money

Psalm 24:1: The earth is the Lord's, and everything in it, the world, and all who live in it....

Philippians 4:19 And my God will meet all your needs according to his glorious riches in Christ Jesus.

Luke 6:38 Give, and it will be given to you. A good measure, pressed down, shaken together and running over, will be poured into your lap. For with the measure you use, it will be measured to you.

Romans 13:8 Let no debt remain outstanding, except the continuing debt to love one another, for he who loves his fellowman has fulfilled the law.

2 Corinthians 9:6–8 Remember this: Whoever sows sparingly will also reap sparingly, and whoever sows generously will also reap generously. Each man should give what he has decided in his heart to give, not reluctantly or under compulsion, for God loves a cheerful giver. And God is able to make all grace abound to you, so that in all things at all times, having all that you need, you will abound in every good work.

Matthew 23:23 You give a tenth of your spices ... but you have neglected the more important matters of the law ... you should have practiced the latter, without neglecting the former.

Prayer for Managing Your Money

God, everything I have belongs to you. You have given me everything I have. I praise you for any income I receive. I thank you for a roof over my head, clothes to wear, and food to eat. God, whatever you bless me with, I present it to you and ask you to bless it and use it for your kingdom. Lord, I pray that what you place in my hands is not mine to keep but to give to bless others and to build your kingdom. Give me wisdom when paying my bills and managing my finances. Show me how to spend wisely. I praise you and I worship you with my income and anything else you bless me with. I give to your kingdom so that others will be blessed. Thank you, God. Amen.

Questions for Thought or Discussion

1. How can I worship God in my giving (money, time, praying for others)?

2. What activities do I participate in that honor God in my finances?

3. What spending habits can I change to save money?

4. What steps can I take immediately to start managing my money as a single person (budget, savings account, credit report)?

CHAPTER 10

Establishing Your Individuality

❧ ♦ ❧

As you start a new life as a single person, you will have the challenge of finding your own individuality. You are no longer Mr. Husband's wife or Mrs. Wife's husband. You are an individual, no longer connected to someone else in marriage. The best way to establish your individuality is to find and fulfill your God-given purpose in life. One of the best things about being single is the ability to fulfill activities associated with your purpose without having to consider a spouse.

Nothing can make you happier than knowing your purpose in life. When you know your purpose, it helps you to withstand the difficult times, because you know there's a greater plan for your life. There's a great sense of fulfillment when you know what your purpose is.

God created every one of us for a reason. Everybody has a divine purpose according to God's plan. God has given each of us a unique personality. When God created us, he equipped each one of us with a gift or gifts that should be used for his service.

Whether you know what your gifts are or not, your main purpose in life is to glorify God. Man was made in God's image to glorify him. Romans 1:6 says we are all called to belong to Jesus Christ. The bible goes on later in the book of Romans to say that we are also obligated to spread the good news of the Gospel of Jesus Christ. So, if you're thinking you really don't know what your purpose in life is, remember, your main purpose is to glorify God and to spread the good news of Jesus Christ.

There's an emptiness you will have until you fill that emptiness by accepting Jesus Christ as your Lord and Savior. One of the reasons some people get hooked on drugs (and sometimes sex) is that they are looking for something or someone to fill an emptiness that they can fill only by accepting Jesus Christ as Lord and Savior of their life. Once you have accepted Jesus as Savior, you may still feel that emptiness at times, when you are not fulfilling your purpose. When you are not actively serving God by serving others with the gifts that God has blessed you with, you will feel incomplete at times.

You will never feel complete joy and peace until you are actively using your God-given gifts. Life may be going great for you, but it could be even greater if you used the special abilities God gave you. You will forever search for that person who makes you feel like a million dollars. You will always have times of discontentment until you begin to participate in service for God.

The question is, "How do I find out what specific service I should be doing for God?" The Bible speaks of numerous gifts and callings. Pray and ask God what your gifts are. Ask God what he would have you to do to help build the body of Christ. We build each other in the body of Christ by using our gifts. Every believer has a part in edifying the body of Christ. Ask God what your part is. After you pray, look for opportunities in your local church. Volunteer for openings and try them out for a while to see if they are a fit for you. God will confirm in your heart where you should be.

I found out what my unique service for God was by accident—or so I thought. I was in a church where each Sunday the children's director asked for volunteers to help teach the children. She made this plea for weeks, but nobody volunteered. One Sunday, I responded to her plea and volunteered to help with the children. The more I worked with them, the more I realized how much I enjoyed it.

It was years later that God confirmed in my heart that teaching is one of my spiritual gifts. One Sunday, as I was teaching a lesson, I sensed an overwhelming sense of approval that this is exactly what I was called to do. It was at that moment that I realized I was fulfilling my purpose. I had never experienced so much fulfillment and peace in my entire life. Once I received the confirmation in my heart that my gift was teaching, nothing could get me down. Receiving this confirmation gave me so much confidence in God's plan for my life. Knowing my purpose put everything else in my life in perspective. I wanted to make sure my decisions and daily activities were in line with what God planned for my life. I try to make sure I don't do anything to compromise the gift he has blessed me with. I constantly work to learn as much as I can so I can impart to others what God teaches me through his word.

Sometimes life's activities can distract you from what you should be doing for God. Financial problems, relationships, family problems, and work can all distract you. When these distractions come, pray and ask God to help you keep your focus on his plan for your life.

When it comes to decision-making, think about your purpose and what type of impact the decision will have on your life. Sometimes loneliness can cause you to make decisions you wouldn't normally make. You just get tired of being alone and are tempted to compromise your values. Sometimes you might even get to the point where you want to go out and participate in things you shouldn't participate in. You want to seek out companionship, or something you know would cause you to feel guilty later. You may even be tempted to go back to an abusive situation that God has delivered you from. You may be tempted to spend time with someone you know is not in God's plan for your life.

Well, compromise is very expensive. How? When you compromise, you are placing yourself in a position where you may not be as effective in your purpose. You should always be prepared to share the Gospel, or at least a testimony of God's goodness with others.

As it says in 1 Peter 3:15–16, "But sanctify the Lord God in your hearts. Always be prepared to give an answer to everyone who asks you to give the reason for the hope that you have. But do this with gentleness and respect, keeping a clear conscience, so that those who speak maliciously against your good behavior in Christ may be ashamed of their slander." The best way to be prepared to help others is by refusing to compromise in any situation.

Know your purpose, fulfill your purpose, and stay focused on your purpose. Allow God's personality to show through your personality as you establish your individuality.

How to Establish Your Individuality

1. **Look closely at yourself and who you are.** Figure out what personality God has given you and work on allowing him to show through your personality. Are you an outgoing person or a more private person? What are your strengths and weaknesses? How do you see yourself? How do others see you? Accept yourself for who you are. Love yourself for who you are. God gave you a unique personality. Be yourself. No one else can be you but you. Work on sharpening your strong areas to make yourself a better person. Work at improving in the areas that could possibly be hurtful to yourself or others.

2. **Get a study guide on the ministry gifts and study. Pray** that God will reveal your purpose and calling as you study the ministry gifts. As you read the descriptions for each of the gifts, which ones remind you of yourself? Which ones do you feel you have already been active in?

3. **Think about and decide what it is you're passionate about and work in that area.** What areas of ministry or church have you always been interested in? Volunteer for those areas to see which one you really feel comfortable doing.

4. **When you find a ministry gift you feel is for you, volunteer to work in that area at church or in the community.** When you become active in it, you will know if this is the direction of your calling. As you participate in that area, you will know in your heart if that is the place for which God has called you.

5. **Say "yes" when you're asked to do things at church or in the community.** When you are asked to volunteer for activities, try it. Don't hesitate to help where it's needed. As you begin to work in that area, you will know if it is the place for you or not. You never know— it might lead to that special ministry God has for you.

Scriptures for Establishing Your Individuality

2 Peter 1:10 Therefore, my brothers, be all the more eager to make your calling and election sure. For if you do these things, you will never fall.

Philippians3:14I press on toward the goal to win the prize for which God has called me heavenward in Christ Jesus.

1 Corinthians 7:20 Let every man abide in the same calling wherein he was called. (KJV)

Romans 11:29 For God's gifts and his call are irrevocable.

Romans 12:6 We have different gifts, according to the grace given us.

1 Corinthians 7:34 There is a difference between a wife and a virgin. The unmarried woman cares about the things of the Lord, that she may be holy both in body and in spirit. But she who is married cares about the things of the world—how she may please her husband. (KJV)

1 Corinthians 12:4–11 There are different kinds of gifts, but the same Spirit. There are different kinds of service, but the same Lord. There are different kinds of working, but the same God works all of them in all men. Now to each one the manifestation of the Spirit is given for the common good. To one there is given through the Spirit the message of wisdom, to another the message of knowledge by means of the same Spirit, to another faith by the same Spirit, to another gifts of healing by that one Spirit, to another miraculous powers, to another prophecy, to another distinguishing between spirits, to another speaking in different kinds of tongues, and to still another the interpretation of tongues. All these are the work of one and the same Spirit, and he gives them to each one, just as he determines.

Prayer for Establishing Your Individuality

Lord, I praise you for creating me in your image. I want to be pleasing to you, Father. I want to fulfill what you have set me on this earth to fulfill. God, I ask that you will reveal to me the thing that you would have me to do. Please show me what it is you want me to do to help build the body of Christ. I want to help someone know you better. Show me what I can do to accomplish that. I yield whatever you have given me to your service. Have your way in my life. I say yes to whatever you want me to do. Lord,

I thank you for the gifts you have given me. I know you have a plan for my life. I don't want to do anything that would interfere with that plan. I want to walk in obedience with your will. Lead me, guide me, and show me the way. Help me to keep my eyes on you. Please keep me from those things and those people who would distract me from what you have for me. Thank you, God. Amen.

Questions for Thought or Discussion

1. How would I describe my personality in three words?

2. What words do people use to describe me?

3. What areas do I need to allow God to strengthen in my personality?

4. What areas do I need God's help to improve in my personality?

5. Read the chapters in the Bible that refer to the gifts of God: 1 Corinthians 12 and Romans 11. Find a study guide that explains each gift. Which gifts remind me of myself when I read them?

6. When requests for volunteers are made in church, which ones am I drawn to the most?

CHAPTER 11

Starting a Devotion Time with God

❧◆❧

D uring a divorce, I cannot express how important devotion time is to your recovery and also your relationship with God. Devotion simply means spending time with God by reading the Bible and praying. Devotion time with God is critical as you seek to deepen and strengthen your relationship with him. The more time you spend with God, the more connected you will be with him. Think of the branches of a tree. If the branches are cut off, they will cease to live. They will die because they are no longer connected to the tree and will not be able to receive what they need to survive. We have to stay connected to God to be able to survive.

Devotion is not Bible study. Bible study is when you are searching and studying the word of God. You usually use dictionaries and commentaries for Bible study. Devotion is not the time or place for Bible study. Devotion is spending time with God in tenderness and intimacy—through prayer, scripture reading, and worship.

Spending time alone with God is by far the most effective way to make it through any day, especially when recovering from a divorce. Jesus is the lover of your soul. He's your heavenly Father. You should spend time with him daily. No one can ever take his place in your life. Nobody will ever treat you as he does. He's the only one who will never fail you. He's the only one you can count on every time.

When I was going through divorce, I was devastated. I felt as if I couldn't go on. However, this experience caused me to realize that I had put too much trust in the relationship and not enough trust in God. I've learned that you have to put your trust in God. Even when it comes to trusting a spouse, you have to trust God to keep him or her. Jesus is someone you can always turn to, no matter what. He's there to hold your hand and help you through any situation. You have to establish a relationship with him that no one will ever be able to come between.

The more time you spend with God in prayer and devotion, the more established your relationship with him will be. You will also be more sensitive to his will and his guidance in your life. The Bible says that God's sheep hear his voice (John 10). As God's sheep, you will be able to recognize God's voice more clearly as you spend time with him. You will be able to sense his comfort throughout the day. You'll sense his presence as you do your daily chores. You will begin to hunger for more and more time with him. Spending time with God pays off in so many ways.

Talking to him and spending time worshiping him is an investment in your spiritual life. Sometimes you may feel that you don't have enough time to devote to God. Often, we wake up in the morning and hit the floor running without acknowledging him. As you honor God with your precious time, it will seem at times that he multiplies your minutes and hours for the rest of the day so that you'll be able to accomplish the things you need to accomplish.

Spending time with God will give you the strength you need to walk in the Spirit throughout the day. Galatians 5:16 says, "Walk in the Spirit and ye shall not fulfill the lust of the flesh" (KJV). As you spend time with God in prayer and Bible reading, he will empower you to walk victoriously and give you the strength to resist temptation. Spending time with God in devotion will help you make better choices because you are in communion with him. You will be able to hear his voice better as you commune and fellowship with him daily. Stay connected with God through devotion time with him.

How to Establish a Devotion Time with God

1. **Find a quiet, solitary place in your home that you can use for your devotion time.** It could be one of the rooms in your house that is seldom used. You can use a room that is always quiet at a certain time of the day. You can use a special chair in your bedroom or place a stool or chair in your bedroom closet. When you select the place you will use for your devotion time, place your Bible, notepad, and a study guide (if you choose to use one) in that place for easy access. Choosing a permanent spot will help you to be consistent in your devotion time.

2. **Pick a quiet time for your devotion.** It may be early in the morning before everyone else awakes. It may be late at night after everyone's gone to bed. Pick a time when things are settled and you can spend time with God with no interruptions. You may want to let everyone know about your devotion time and place to limit interruptions, especially if you have children.

3. **Keep a prayer list of people to pray for to help you start your prayer.** As you talk to people who ask you to pray for them, keep a record of their names and prayer requests. Add their names to your prayer list and pray for them during your devotion time. This guarantees that you will always have something to pray about. You can always pray for the nation, the world leaders, and salvation for those who don't know Jesus.

4. **Make a list of three or four songs to sing during your devotion time.** You don't have to be a great singer. The purpose of the songs is to create an atmosphere of worship and intimacy before you begin your prayer. You can sing one song each time. You don't have to sing an entire song, and you don't have to sing for a long time. Just sing a few lines of a simple song to God from your heart. It will make a difference in your time with him.

5. **Select the scriptures you will read ahead of time so you don't have to spend time looking for something to read during your actual devotion time.** Find the scriptures you will read and place a bookmark in your Bible. Read the scriptures and meditate on them, allowing the words to settle in your heart. Try to keep them in mind as you go through the day or as you lie in bed before going to sleep. There are myriad devotional books out there. Visit the local Christian

bookstore to find one you like. There are also Web sites you can visit to download and print devotionals free of charge.

6. **Decide on a period for your devotion time.** Your devotion time should last as long as you like. There is no standard timeframe for devotion. It's your personal time with God. Start with a duration that's realistic for you. The length of time will be different for everyone and will probably be different every time for you. It could be anywhere from five to fifteen minutes or more. Don't limit your time or try to stretch it out longer than the time you've allotted. Just use that time to focus only on God.

7. **Spend your devotion time with God with a song, prayer, and scripture in the order that comes natural for you.** Your devotion time may look something like this:

6:00 am	Opening prayer and prayer for others on your prayer list
6:05 am	Worship song
6:10 am	Scripture
6:15 am	Closing prayer

As you pray, remember that you are spending time with God not only to talk to him but also to listen to what he may have to say to you. Prayer is a two-way communication. Talk to God as if he were a friend sitting there listening to you. You can sing aloud or sing silently to God. It doesn't matter how you sound. Sing from your heart in worship to God. Read the scriptures you selected to read for devotion. The scriptures will help keep you focused during this time. Open your heart to God and allow him to minister to you during that time. To allow God to minister to you, ask yourself, "What does this scripture mean for me today?" Then listen with your heart.

8. **Commit to your devotion time with God.** Pray and ask God to give you the strength and discipline to spend time with him each day. Pray that you will hunger and thirst for time with him. Don't give up or beat yourself up if you miss a day or two. Just keep trying—the more you do it, the more you will be drawn to your devotion time and place naturally. The more you commit to your regularly scheduled time for devotion, the more it will become a natural part of your life.

Scriptures for Starting a Devotion Time with God

Psalms5:3 In the morning, O LORD, you hear my voice; in the morning I lay my requests before you and wait in expectation.

Acts 3:19 When the times of refreshing shall come from the presence of the Lord. (KJV)

Matthew 5:6 Blessed are those who hunger and thirst for righteousness, for they will be filled.

Psalms 1:1–2 Blessed is the man who does not walk in the counsel of the wicked or stand in the way of sinners or sit in the seat of mockers. But his delight is in the law of the LORD, and on his law he meditates day and night.

Joshua 1:8 Do not let this Book of the Law depart from your mouth; meditate on it day and night, so that you may be careful to do everything written in it. Then you will be prosperous and successful.

Mark 1:35 Very early in the morning, while it was still dark, Jesus got up, left the house and went off to a solitary place, where he prayed.

Prayer for Starting a Devotion Time with God

Lord, I thank you for the privilege of being able to come before your presence in prayer. I am honored that you want to spend time with me. I love you and adore you for who you are in my life. Lord, I ask that you remind me to spend time with you when I am in a hurry. Give me a hunger and thirst for more of you. Lord, I have set aside a time just for you, and I pray that you will bless this time and keep it only for you. I want to know your will for my life.

I want to know you better and get closer to you. Speak to me through your word; touch my heart, mind, and spirit as I spend this time with you. Give me divine direction and wisdom as I serve you each day of my life. Make me more like you. Help me depend on you for every single thing in my life. I trust you, Lord, to see me through each day. Thank you for watching over me and for being there with me every minute, even when I don't feel that you are there. I love you, Lord. Amen.

Questions for Thought or Discussion

1. What's the quietest time of the day in my home?

2. What's the best place in my home for quiet time for prayer and spending time alone with God?

3. How will staying connected to God through devotion time help me through divorce?

4. How will spending time alone with God help me daily?

CHAPTER 12

Approaching the Dating Scene

❧◆❧

So, you are now ready to start dating. As you approach the dating scene, remember that the main purpose of dating is to determine if the person you are dating is a potential marriage partner. If it is not your desire to marry, then you probably have a different reason for dating. Maybe you just want to meet new friends. The focus of this chapter is to address those who are dating in hope of starting a serious relationship.

Many singles date casually with no specific goal in mind. Dating with no specific goals could cause the relationship to move endlessly with no clear marks of progress. It could also cause misunderstanding or confusion about individual goals for the relationship. While you are dating, you should have a specific goal.

For those of you who are dating in hope of marriage, it's important to know that for each person you date, your goal is to get to know each other to see if you will be able to help each other fulfill your purposes in life. Your personalities, lifestyles, values, and levels of commitment should support both of your goals.

This doesn't mean that you are interviewing or interrogating each person you go out with. It means you are selective about whom to go out with. Selective dating means choosing carefully who you will spend your valuable time with. You are using your time wisely and making the most of someone else's time. If it is not your desire to marry, it's important that you tell the person you are going out with as early as possible. Make sure you are aware of each other's intentions as you get acquainted. That person might be praying for and looking for a spouse. If it's not your desire to marry, you need to let her know so that she won't have false hope for a serious relationship with you.

I met a man once who, by our third date, told me that his plans were to marry within the next year. He had never been married and was determined to marry soon. I told him that I was in no hurry to remarry.

Because I want to be extra careful the next time I marry, I want to take time to get to know someone. Even though I made this clear, every time we talked he would mention marriage and what a wonderful wife I would be for him. I had a hard time getting to know him, because he talked so much about his desire to marry instead of relaxing and allowing me to get to know him.

At another time, I went out with a man whom I really enjoyed talking to and spending time with. After a few dates, I asked him where he stood in regard to relationships. He said his plans were to get himself together financially before getting into a serious relationship with anyone. He made it very clear that he was not looking for a commitment. He just wanted to make new friends. However, by the third time we went out, he began to talk about getting physical. He talked about being "friends with benefits." I made it clear to him that "friends with benefits" is not a lifestyle I desire. The dates with him didn't last long after that conversation.

If it becomes clear that your intentions are different from the intentions of the person you're dating, do something about it. Don't play games. Ladies, don't give your body to someone who isn't ready for commitment. Gentlemen, don't spend a lot of time and money on someone who has made it clear that she's not looking for a serious relationship. Be very careful not to get involved in a "friends with benefits" relationship. Someone can get hurt emotionally in this type of affair, because you run the risk of one person wanting more than the other person desires to give.

The joy in dating is the opportunity to meet new people and possibly make new friends. However, remember to keep things in perspective as you make new acquaintances. Take time to evaluate each person you meet. Don't rush into a serious relationship without getting to know the person first.

Before you can determine if the person you are dating is a potential marriage partner, you have to know yourself first. It's best if you have taken some time to think about who you are and where you're headed in life. Taking an inventory of your life and who you are will help you see what you have to offer someone else in a relationship.

Here are some basic questions to ask yourself as you think about entering into another relationship:

- Am I clear of any attachments to my past relationship (i.e., am I legally divorced, not just separated)?

- Have I let go of the past and am I open to what God has in store for my future?

- What role did I play in the breakdown of my last relationship and how have I resolved those issues?

- What are some positive attributes I can bring to a relationship?

- Do I know what a Godly relationship looks like and am I ready spiritually, emotionally, and physically to have one?

- Am I ready to trust someone else in another relationship? If not, what do I need to do to prepare myself to be able to trust again?

Make sure you have thoroughly answered these questions and you know for sure that you are ready to start dating.

Let's talk about how to approach the dating scene. More than likely, things have changed since you last dated. You've been married a little while or maybe for many years, and you're wondering how to get back into dating. The best way to approach the dating scene is with an open heart for what God wants for you. God has a divine plan for your life and is ordering your every footstep. Having an open heart means being open to whatever God has for you, even if it means being single for the rest of your life.

One thing the Bible is very clear on is that we are not to be yoked unequally with unbelievers (2 Corinthians 6:14). Remember this as you think about dating. Don't date people you know are not believers in Christ Jesus as the son of God. Your fellowship together will not be as unified as it would be with someone who holds the same beliefs. You may have some basic things in common, but at some point, you may not be able to walk in agreement in your walk with Christ. Your life priorities may be different. Your values and standards may be different. Some of the differences may seem small while you are dating, but some issues tend to magnify when you marry, because you are now much closer to the issues. When you are dating someone who is a believer, it's typically easier to handle issues, because both of you are in a relationship with God and are able to talk to your heavenly Father about each other. This does not mean you won't have problems with someone who is a believer. Chances are greater that person will be sensitive to God's guidance more so than someone who does not believe in God.

Paul stated in the Bible that he wishes everyone would remain single like him. He continued by saying that he realizes, though, that everyone has their own gifts from God and that not everyone has the gift of being single. He even went on to say later that if you cannot control yourself, you should get married (1 Corinthians 7:7–9). If you know in your heart that you do not have the gift of being single, ask God for guidance as you pray for a husband or wife. Don't marry the first person you date because you feel you can't control yourself. Don't settle for someone you know you would not be completely happy with merely to satisfy your desires. Pray for God's direction in going into marriage with someone.

Make sure you are ready for remarriage as you begin the dating process. If sex is the only reason you want to be married, remember that marriage does not take away your lack of self-control. Managing self-control is not the purpose for marriage. Self-control is something you need to learn how to manage before you get married. Pray and ask God to help you with this as you date.

Jesus comes to give us life and life abundantly. He desires for you to live a fulfilling life. For this reason, you have to pray before you go out with anyone. Before you begin dating, ask God for guidance as to whom you should and should not go out with. Pray for God to show you if this person is part of his plan for your abundant life. By praying this prayer, you will be prepared to watch your date's personality to see if this is someone whom God would want you to have in your life.

God allows people into our lives for different reasons. Ask yourself when you go out on your date, "Will this person be a hindrance or help for God's plan for my abundant living?" "Has this person entered my life to be a good friend or a lifetime mate?" As you date, pray and ask yourself these questions. The only way you'll know this for sure is to pray about it.

God answers prayers. When you earnestly pray, with an open heart and ear, he will answer you. Once God reveals the answer, there won't be any doubt. So, watch and pray with every person you go out with. Once you determine that this person is or is not a help for God's plan for your life, you must decide whether to continue to go out with him or her.

Before we talk about how to approach that first date, let's look at a few things you should be cautious about. Wasting time is a big problem I see with many single people. I am speaking in reference to wasting time with people of the opposite sex that you know you will not marry or don't even like. Going to dinner with someone you don't like. Spending hours on the phone with someone in whom you've seen red flags. The danger of spending time with someone you know is not for you is that one of you could become emotionally attached. Be careful about how much time you spend with someone you don't want to get serious with. Don't mislead anyone.

The time that you are spending with someone you don't want to be serious with could be used preparing yourself for meeting the right person. Every minute of your life should be spent working toward God's purpose for your life in one way or another. If you know the person you are spending time with is not in God's purpose for your life, you are wasting precious time. I'm not talking about someone you have just met and are beginning to date, getting to know this person and praying the Lord's will for the relationship. I'm talking about the person you've had time to get to know, you've prayed about for a relationship, and you know is not in God's will for your life. You're not attracted to this person. He doesn't have the qualities you want from the person you will spend the rest of your life with. This is the person you are wasting time with. You could be using that time to develop yourself and prepare yourself for the person God has for you.

Don't spend time with someone because you are lonely, or to get a free meal, or because you have nothing else to do. I know a lady who met a man on a blind date. She immediately recognized that he was not someone with whom she would want a serious relationship. However, anytime this man asked her out, she would go out with him. I asked her why she continued to see him when she knew he was not someone she would want to get serious with. She told me she did it for the free dinners. I thought, "Wow, do you not have enough money to buy your own dinner?" Not only was she wasting her time, but she was also wasting his time and money.

Be wise and careful about how you use your time. Don't waste someone's time or money when you know that person is not someone you want a future with. Be careful that you are not engaging that person's heart by spending time with him or her or having lengthy conversations on the telephone when you know that person is not the one for you. There are more productive ways you could use your time. You could spend more time in prayer for your future. You could spend more time doing things for other people. Don't waste a single moment.

Another big mistake many singles make is opening their heart to someone they shouldn't open their heart to. Singles oftentimes become emotionally connected to someone they should not connect with. There are many examples of such relationships:

- A girl who begins to fall in love with a man who told her in the beginning of the friendship that he is not interested in being anything more than friends

- A guy who pretends to want only friendship from a girl but at the same time hopes and prays for a relationship with her, falling for her in the process

- A girl who confides in a married co-worker and begins to fall in love with him because he's so caring and so encouraging

- A married man who falls in love with another woman because she's very attentive, exciting, and flattering

- A single woman who gets caught up in conversations with a married man who shows her attention she desires so badly

Getting emotionally connected to someone is something that can happen to you before you even realize it's happening; and by the time you realize it, it's too late.

Proverbs 4:23 says, "Above all else, guard your heart, for it is the wellspring of life." Guarding your heart in the context of single life means watching and being careful about who you allow to enter your life and your heart. The more time you spend with someone, enjoying conversations and friendly exchanges, the more you are allowing this person to enter your heart.

Your heart is composed of your mind, your will, and your emotions. Connecting to someone emotionally and mentally causes you to connect with him or her on a very deep level. That's why when you engage in intimate conversations with someone, your thoughts tend to become more and more consumed with that person. You can't stop thinking about her. The problem with this is that it's with someone you shouldn't be connected to—a married man, a married woman, someone who has told you they do not want a relationship with you, your ex-spouse that you've decided not to reunite with. These are relationships and conversations that shouldn't happen.

You should not be emotionally connected to someone else's spouse. You should not allow yourself to fall in love with someone who has already told you that he doesn't want you.

So, how do you avoid this? You avoid this by guarding your heart. Take every precaution to limit conversations or associations with people you know you should not be emotionally connected to. Keep distance between you and those with whom you foresee possible inappropriate connection.

A single woman should not have frequent and engaging conversations with a married man. It's too risky. The risk is that one or both of you will begin to have feelings that shouldn't be there. It could happen to anyone. Don't ever think you're too strong and that it wouldn't happen to you. This is something you would probably never do intentionally. But it can happen if you engage in conversations you should not engage in.

The loneliness you feel or the desire to feel wanted by someone can sometimes cause you to fall into situations you shouldn't get in to. However, you are responsible for your decisions regardless of your circumstances. You should always be watchful and prayerful with relationships to make sure you are honoring God.

The hard part about becoming emotionally connected to the wrong person is that it's very painful when you finally realize you can't be with that person. Even when there is no sex or any physical contact involved, it's still painful. It may not be as painful as divorce, but it hurts when you lose someone you're connected to. You miss talking to that person. You miss spending time with that person. You miss sharing with and confiding in that person. You have to go through a healing process when the tie is broken.

So, guard your heart. Be careful with your relationships. Watch and observe your conversations and visits to make sure you're not getting involved where you shouldn't. Take your time getting to know that person and what she wants before you fall head over heels. Consistently pray about every single association and relationship. Don't spend too much time with someone you already know is not a potential marriage partner. Spend your time seeking God and preparing yourself for your next relationship.

Now that you know what you need to watch out for, let's talk about dating. People date for different reasons. Some date casually with no intent of ever committing to anyone. Some date with the desire to marry. Make sure that as you date, your intentions are clear with the other person. Whenever the subject of relationships comes up, be sure to let them know how you feel about dating and what your goal for a relationship is. If your intention is to casually date with no intention of commitment, let them know so they won't expect anything more. If you desire a mate and eventually a God-given marriage, let them know to make sure they desire the same. Make sure your actions don't say something different than what your words are saying. You want to ensure you are on the same page with them in regard to dating to help maintain a clear understanding throughout the relationship.

Take your time when dating. Don't rush into a serious relationship right away, especially if you are recently divorced. Give yourself time to get to know yourself and get a feel for what's going on around you.

To begin meeting people, get out of the house and get involved in activities you enjoy doing. As you get involved in things you enjoy, you will likely meet someone who enjoys doing the same activities. I enjoy going to see movies at the theatre. When I'm at the theatre, I like to stand around and look at the posters. Once I was in the lobby of a movie theatre looking at posters and I met a man who was also looking at the posters. We chatted for a while and found we had some things in common. We ended up exchanging phone numbers and becoming longtime friends.

I've also met men while at the grocery store, post office, and singles activities at church.

As you go out to run errands or to participate in various activities, put on your friendly face. If it's your desire to meet someone, make sure you look presentable anytime you leave the house. To make yourself available for dating, you have to make sure your appearance is attractive anytime you go anywhere. Always look nice when you visit the grocery store, gas station, bookstore, or wherever you go, even if it's just a short visit. You never know when you'll meet someone. Looking presentable does not mean you have to wear your best suit or dress every time you go out. If you're running errands, wear a decent, clean pair of jeans with a nice shirt. You could even wear a jogging suit.

Gentlemen, make sure your hair is clean and neat and that your face is well-groomed. Don't be afraid to say "hi" if you see a woman you like. Don't go overboard by being pushy. Just let them know you are interested and available. You can do all this with something as simple as eye contact. As you approach each other, give her a friendly look and say, "Hi." If you have the opportunity to chat, try to get a feel for her personality to see if you'd like to get to know her better.

Ladies, you could wear a sundress with sandals. You could also wear a shirt and pair of jeans or a jogging suit. You don't have to wear full makeup. Just put on some lip gloss to add a little shine to your lips and pull your hair back into a neat style or ponytail. When you are out and you notice someone looking at you, let him know you are available if he looks like someone you would be interested in. Let him know you're available by smiling at him with your eyes. As you talk to him, try to determine if he is someone you would feel comfortable spending time with. If you feel comfortable doing so, it's okay to exchange numbers. Just make sure you're clear on the best time to call if you have limitations on that. If he asks and you're not comfortable giving your number, ask him if you can have his number instead. One thing I've heard guys say over and over is that they hate it when a woman gives him the wrong number or takes his number and doesn't call. If you don't want to talk to him, let him know at that time. Don't tell him you're going to call if you don't intend to call. Don't give the wrong number. Just let him know politely that you'd rather not exchange numbers. You can say something like, "To be honest with you, I'd rather not exchange numbers right now." He will appreciate your honesty instead of you leading him to think that you will call or giving the wrong number. Put yourself in his shoes and show respect.

From what I've heard men say, it takes a lot for them to even approach you for your number because of the fear of rejection. Don't make it harder for them. Be politely honest and upfront.

Remember your goal for dating as you have conversations with the people you meet. Make sure you are spending your time wisely as you talk on the phone. We tend to spend hours on the phone when we first meet someone. The conversations tend to flow late into the midnight hour as we get to know somebody new. Try to manage your time wisely as you meet new friends. Don't be in a hurry to learn everything at once.

Let's say you've talked several times on the phone and you decide to go out for a date. You both have determined that you'd like to get to know each other better and you want to see each other. You set a dinner date for Friday night.

It's Friday night, and you're getting ready to go out. Let's look at some very basic things to think about for your date (for both men and women):

Do's for a New Date

- Shower and wear a nice outfit to look and smell fresh and clean. You want to make your best impression. (I shouldn't have to say this, but I felt I needed to, since I went out once with a guy who smelled like cheese. Yuk!)

- For safety purposes, especially for single parents, for the first date, meet him or her at the location you're visiting (restaurant, theatre, etc.). You shouldn't meet at your house until you get to know each other better. You want to make sure you establish an understanding about visiting each other's homes before your date knows where you live.

- Gentlemen, always give a small bouquet of flowers or another type of small gift on the first date. It shows the woman that you were anticipating your time with her. Make sure the gift is practical and not a weird or expensive gift.

I had a date with a guy who brought a framed picture of himself on the second date. I thought this was a little presumptuous and a little weird.

- Gentlemen, always pay for the first date. This shows plain old-fashioned chivalry and that you want to take care of your lady. On future dates, you can allow her to pay if and only if she offers to pay.

- Ladies, give a small gift as a gesture of appreciation for the nice time you will have that evening. Some ideas for gifts are a nice CD or a book.

- Ladies, be flexible. Don't be fussy on your date. If he asks, it's okay to mention preferences, but don't insist on having your way with everything.

- Have fun. This is a time to relax and enjoy the opportunity to meet someone new. This person might become a lifetime friend. Enjoy getting to know him or her. Be natural and relaxed. Show your friendly side and let the other person see your pleasant personality. This is not the time to play detective or security guard. You are there to get to know each other and to have fun doing so.

- Always make an effort to give a good impression, but at the same time, make sure you are being yourself. Be natural. Your date wants to see the real you.

- Keep the conversation light. Try not to get into any intense discussions or controversial subjects. Pace the conversation to allow for a nice and comfortable visit.

- Call and thank your date afterwards to let him know you appreciate the time. Let her know you enjoyed the date if you did. This lets the person you dated know you look forward to spending more time with him or her.

Don'ts for a New Date

- Don't be late. Being late could send the message that the date is not important to you. Gentlemen, if you are picking her up, don't be early—you don't want to catch her with the hot curlers in her hand.

- Ladies, don't be picky or fussy on your dates. Don't fuss at the waiter if your order is not perfect. Don't complain about the food. The purpose of the date is to get to know each other. Don't spend your time complaining about trivial things. Be pleasant and elegant.

- Don't talk about your past relationships. Talking about your failed marriage or past relationships sets a negative tone for the date. It also sends the message that you may still be holding on to that person and not really interested in your date.

  - Don't ask too many personal questions on the first date. You don't want the date to seem like an interrogation or an invasion of privacy. You will find out some things through observation without having to ask. Take your time to get to know your date without asking too many questions upfront.

  - Don't tell lies to impress your date. If your date asks a question you don't feel comfortable answering yet, just let him or her know you'd rather not discuss it at this point. Be prepared to discuss it at the appropriate time later. If you tell lies, it creates distrust in the relationship when the truth is finally revealed.

  - Don't do anything you wouldn't normally do to impress your date. Be yourself and be natural to allow the other person to see the real you. You should be on your best behavior to make a good first impression, but you should not do anything that is totally against your personality to impress someone. Don't talk about marriage. Mentioning marriage on a first date could lead your date to think you are in a hurry to get married without even getting to know him or her first. Marriage is a topic that should eventually be discussed to make sure you are on the same page with the person you're in a relationship with; however, it's not something that should be discussed on a first date unless the other person brings it up.

After the Date

Let's say it's the day after and you're thinking about the date last night. You're either glowing from having such a good time or you're sulking because you're disappointed with how things went. If you still want to continue seeing this person after your first date, that's a good sign. Most people know right away if they'd like to see their date again. Either there's a spark of interest or there's not. Either there's a connection or it's not. Don't feel bad if there is no connection. It's not the end of the world if you realize on the first date that this is not the mate for you. Your ultimate goal is to be in a relationship that is sanctioned by God. If the relationship does not work out, it just means that there is someone else out there who is better for you.

Gentlemen, if you've determined after the date that you definitely do not ever want to see her again, you need to let her know as soon as possible. Don't tell her you're going to call and then not call; it wouldn't leave a good impression. Remember, you don't want to waste anybody's time. I would advise you to pray about it first and then have a discussion with her about what you are thinking. Don't leave her hanging.

Don't make her wonder what went wrong and why you never called. Let her know why you're feeling the way you feel. Tell her that you have decided to move on. Be politely honest and upfront with her.

Ladies, the same applies to you. If you feel after the date that he is definitely not the guy for you, let him know. Don't leave him hanging. When he calls, let him know that you appreciate the nice evening but that you're not interested in going out with him again. He will appreciate your honesty.

If after the date you decide you do want to see this person again, that's great. There's a chance for a new friendship or relationship here. As you talk to this person, continue to pray and ask for God's guidance for the relationship. *Is this to be a serious relationship or a friendship?* Ask God where he wants this relationship to go. Be watchful for the tone and direction of the conversations. Make sure you're headed in the same direction and at the same pace. Sometimes one person can jump far ahead of the other person because someone's not communicating his or her feelings. Keep communication open and honest.

As you approach the dating scene, pray and ask God to help you manage your relationships. Marriage should represent the kingdom of God and his awesome love. As you meet people and seek to determine if they can be a life partner for you, make sure they can help you represent God's love and righteousness to the world.

How to Approach the Dating Scene

1. **Pray and ask God to lead and direct you through the dating process.** Ask God to give you wisdom and discernment so you can identify those who would be healthy for you. Ask him to put a roadblock before anyone who would be unhealthy for you. Prepare your heart, mind, and spirit to accept who God has for you. God knows you better than you know yourself. He knows what is good for you. Trust God to match you with the right one. He's the best matchmaker this world could ever know.

2. **Take an inventory of your life and who you are to determine what you have to offer someone else in a relationship.** Make sure you are ready to get involved with someone else. Make sure you have moved past the emotional phases of the divorce—anger, grief, low self-esteem. You don't want to take any emotional baggage into the next relationship. You should be in a healthy state of mind and capable of getting to know someone new with no emotional reservations.

3. **Make a list of your have-to-haves and nice-to-haves for the other person.** No, there is nothing wrong with having a list. Of course, God's plan for you could supersede your list, but it doesn't hurt to know in your mind what it is you desire in a mate. God can give you the desires of your heart. As you pray for guidance, God will send the right person your way, whether he has the qualities on your list or not. Lists are good reference points when you're not sure about whether to take dating to the next level with a potential partner. If you're dating someone you're unsure about, look at your list and compare that person's qualities to what's on your list and pray about whether she is the right one. Then decide whether the relationship is one you want to pursue.

   Your have-to-haves are those qualities the other person must have that are vital to your spiritual, mental, physical, and financial wellbeing. These are your necessities. For example, a good have-to-have is faith in Jesus Christ. Your spiritual being is critical for your life, so dating someone who is a Christian is important. Another good example of a have-to-have is financial stability. Money management is a big part of a successful marriage, so you want to marry someone who is financially stable and has a history of good money management.

   Nice-to-haves are extra benefits for the relationship. These things add even more to your spiritual, mental, physical, and financial wellbeing.

An example of a nice-to-have for a woman might be a man who is tall, dark, and handsome. For men, a nice-to-have might be a woman who is beautiful with long hair and a nice shape. These qualities are nice-to-haves because they are not vital to your overall wellbeing.

4. **Gentlemen, pray that God will prepare you to be the husband you are to be for your wife.** Submit yourself to God by trusting him to work on your personality so you can be the head of the household that you are to be. Read the second and third chapters of Genesis to see how God created Adam and gave him the role of leadership. Read the fifth chapter of Ephesians to review the husband's role in the home. Pray and ask God to prepare you to be the man and husband you should be *before* you get married.

5. **Ladies, pray that God will prepare you to be the wife you are to be for your husband.** You'll see by reading the second chapter of Genesis that Eve was created to be a helper suitable for Adam. Likewise, wives should be helpers for their husbands. Read Proverbs 31:10–31 to get ideas for how to be a godly woman. Read the fifth chapter of Ephesians to review the wife's role in the home. Pray and ask God to manifest the qualities you have that would make you a suitable wife. Trust him to prepare you for whomever he has for you. Get rid of anything in your personality or your life that could stop you from being a helper for your husband. Before you marry is the time to get yourself together.

Scriptures for Approaching the Dating Scene

1 Corinthians 7:6–9 I wish that all men were as I am. But each man has his own gift from God; one has this gift, another has that. Now to the unmarried and the widows I say: It is good for them to stay unmarried, as I am. But if they cannot control themselves, they should marry, for it is better to marry than to burn with passion.

2 Corinthians 6:14 Do not be yoked together with unbelievers. For what do righteousness and wickedness have in common? Or what fellowship can light have with darkness?

Proverbs 3:5–6 Trust in the LORD with all your heart and lean not on your own understanding; in all your ways acknowledge him, and he will make your paths straight.

Prayer for Approaching the Dating Scene

Lord, I know you have a plan for my life and you know what's best for me. I trust you to lead me and guide me as I begin to date again. I pray for healthy and edifying friendships. I pray that you will keep me from anyone who would harm me or hinder my relationship with you. I pray that you will make me the man/woman I should be. If there's anything about me that would hurt anyone else, I pray that you will remove it from my personality.

Show me how to be the man/woman of God that I should be. Help me to stay pure in my relationships. Give me abundant and joyful living as I meet new people. Show me those who are to be my friends and help me to maintain that level of friendship and not move into something more than it should be. Sanctify all my relationships and help me to glorify your name and let your love show with everyone I meet. Amen.

Questions for Thought or Discussion

1. What steps have I taken to prepare myself mentally, physically, and spiritually for another relationship?

2. Do I want to remarry? Why or why not?

3. What have I learned about myself through this divorce that I need to improve to help me in my next relationship?

4. What do I have to offer someone else to help them fulfill their purpose in life?

5. Will the personality of the person I'm dating connect with my personality to create a godly and righteous representation of God's kingdom and his love?

CHAPTER 13

Resisting Sexual Temptation

ॐ◆ॐ

After loneliness, sexual temptation is probably the biggest struggle
most singles face. There are three points I'd like to make about
sexual temptation that will help you tremendously if you capture
what I say about each point.

First, when you are used to being sexually active, sexual temptation
is generally hard to resist. Your body will crave that activity once it is
gone. You will yearn to get physical from time to time. This is one of the
reasons sexual temptation is hard to resist.

Second, sexual temptation is generally hard to resist because you
want what you cannot have. The reason sex is hard to resist when you are
single is because you know you're not supposed to have sex outside of
marriage, according to the Bible.

You know in your heart and mind that as a Christian single, the Bible
forbids you to indulge in sex outside of marriage. Sex outside of marriage
is called fornication or premarital sex, and it's one thing that the Bible
clearly speaks against. It's one thing we cannot dismiss, saying, "Oh, I
didn't know it was wrong." The Bible clearly states that sex outside of
marriage is forbidden (Ephesians 5:3; Colossians 3:5; 1 Corinthians 6:18–
19), yet you want to do it. You want what you cannot have.

Women like men who don't like them. They don't like the guys who
like them. Some women want men who already have girlfriends or who
are married. Some married men flirt with women. Our ex suddenly
becomes more appealing after the divorce. Some men like women they
can't easily have.

There's actually a scientific explanation for it all. There is a trait
ingrained in our human physiology. Levels of dopamine, the "pleasure"

chemical in the brain, actually increase the longer it takes a pleasure to be fulfilled.

In other words, the longer you have to yearn for someone you can't have, the more pleasurable the whole experience becomes.

So, the more you see someone you know you can't have, the more the "pleasure" chemical in your brain increases. It feels good to a married man when he flirts with someone he knows he can't have. It feels good for a woman to want a man she knows doesn't like her. It feels good to a man when he chases a woman who is not easy to get. There's a thrill in the forbidden. There's a thrill in the chase.

Third, you cannot resist sexual temptation on your own. Resisting is something you can do only with God's help. You have to allow God to be your strength and to be strong through you. You have to submit yourself to him to allow him to control your desires.

Therefore, there are physical, mental, and spiritual reasons why sexual temptation is difficult to resist. Physically, your body is missing a pleasure it once had. Mentally, you want it even more because you're not supposed to have it. Spiritually, it's hard because you can't resist on your own without God's help. For these three reasons, it's inevitable that you will encounter sex-ual temptation.

Now that we've discovered why sexual temptation is so strong, let's talk about how to resist it. Let's look at how temptation starts and the series of actions that occur when you experience it. Being aware of the temptation pro-cess will help you identify when it is happening and how to resist it. Adam and Eve's experience in Genesis 3 will help you understand these series of actions.

Let's look closely at the three steps in Eve's fall. Each of these steps represents the series of actions that occur when you are tempted.

First, Eve listened to and dwelled on the temptation. When the devil tempted Eve, she chose to listen and dwell upon the temptation in deep thought. She listened to every word the devil was saying to her. She dwelled on the lies he was telling her. This is where it begins—in your thoughts. You see somebody beautiful and you allow thoughts to enter your head. You imagine things.

What Eve should have done is managed her thoughts. She should have changed the thoughts of temptation to God's word. She should've dismissed and cast down the thoughts of temptation and not let them dwell in her mind. In the same way, when you encounter the initial thoughts of temptation, you shouldn't dwell on it. Ladies, stop thinking about how handsome that man is.

Gentlemen, don't dwell on how nice that woman's body is. Dismiss those thoughts from your mind and replace them with something godly. Replace those thoughts with scripture or a prayer. The more you think about it, the more the "pleasure" chemical in your brain increases.

When you are having sexual thoughts about someone, switch your thoughts to something else.

Second, Eve looked at the forbidden fruit. Looking indicates that you are concentrating your interest in something. Looking can lead to imagination and infatuation. Looking can lead to cravings of sin and lust of the eyes. Looking can cause you to begin desiring something you shouldn't have. It can cause you to be dragged away and enticed. It can move you to perform actions in your head that you shouldn't perform. What Eve should have done is look away from the temptation. If necessary, you should turn your head and move away from what tempts you. It may be necessary to remove yourself from the vicinity of that person, if possible.

Third, Eve ate the fruit. She thought about it. She looked at it and was enticed by it. She gave in to it. She sinned. And when sin is full grown, it brings birth to death.

Don't give in to sin. Watch the process. Manage your thoughts. Change your thoughts. Don't keep looking. Turn your head. Walk away.

One of the trickiest things God ever gave us was the freedom of choice. In the Garden of Eden, he told Adam and Eve they were free to eat from any tree in the garden; but they could not eat from the tree of the knowledge of good and evil. The good part is we're free to choose what we want, within boundaries. The bad part is that sometimes we make the wrong choices. This is particularly true when we find ourselves in a situation where we're tempted to sin.

Sometimes you'll find yourself in a compromising situation in which you have an opportunity to fulfill your desires by having sex. You might find yourself in a position where you are alone with someone whom you are attracted to and the temperature's rising. You might even intentionally get in situations with someone because you want to. You might find yourself attracted to someone and just want to give in. Even at times like this, you still have an opportunity to choose not to yield to your desires. There is always a way of escape. The Holy Spirit always comes to give you a way out. It's at that point that you have to decide whether to say yes to the Holy Spirit or yes to your desires.

When you have trouble resisting sex, it would be wise to stay away from places or people who tempt you to sin. This is a rule you should follow with anything that tempts you. If alcohol is a temptation for you, stay away from bars or places that are known for serving liquor. Stay away from people who drink. If gossip is something you have a hard time resisting, stay away from people who gossip. If illegal drugs tempt you, stay away from settings known for having drugs around. Proverbs 4:15 says, "Avoid it, pass not by it, turn from it and pass away" (KJV). In other words, don't go anywhere near the things that tempt you to do wrong.

At a point in my life I decided I would no longer date. I concluded that this was the best way for me to avoid sexual temptation. I decided I would only go out with men in group settings with other friends. I found that this is actually a great way to get to know someone. When you date in group settings, not only are you able to get to know the person individually but your friends are also able to observe things you may not see.

I have found that dating in group settings is a safe way to form a relationship with someone without the risk of sexual temptation. This is especially helpful when you are dating someone you are physically attracted to. If you know that person makes you weak in the knees, stay out of compromising situations with him or her. Don't spend too much time alone with that person you are physically attracted to and having trouble resisting.

Set boundaries for the relationship. Boundaries are limitations regarding how much time you will spend alone and limitations on activities that may cause you to be tempted to sin. Having boundaries are very important. Set boundaries early in the relationship so that your guidelines will already be set. Setting guidelines early on will help you avoid getting into tight situations.

One good boundary or guideline to start with is not spending too much private time alone with just the two of you. It's difficult (and illegal) to get intimate in public. Having plans that involve being in group settings will help prevent the temptation to give in to your desire. Sit down and talk about boundaries and make a list—yes, write them down and make sure you both agree on the boundaries.

Make a commitment to stick to your guidelines. Make a commitment to respect each other and show each other affection in ways that are appropriate for dating. This is easier to do when you are in a relationship with someone who has the same goal of purity that you do. Resisting sexual temptation is difficult for most singles, but it's even harder when you're in a relationship with someone who has the attitude that he can do whatever, whenever, and has no desire to try to practice self-control. Make sure you both agree about your commitment to stay pure until marriage.

Of course, you cannot stay pure on your own without God's help, but it does help when you have someone else with the same commitment to depend on God for help in this area.

You can receive the help you need to resist temptation by feeding your spiritual man. You feed your spiritual man by reading the Bible and by praying. "The flesh lusteth against the Spirit, and the spirit against the flesh and these are the contrary one to another" (Galatians 5:17 KJV). What you feed most will be stronger and more likely to win. So, you have to feed your spirit in order to be victorious over temptation. To feed the spirit, read and meditate on God's word every day. Spend time with God by praying and reading the Bible so that he will be there with you to give you strength when needed.

Since the spirit and the flesh war against one another, you can't feed your flesh; you have to starve it so it will not have any power to fight. You have to starve the flesh by not watching or reading things that will increase the desire to want to sin. Your conversation must be holy and not of a sexual nature. Reading God's word, praying, and avoiding conversation and activities of a sexual nature is how you strengthen your spirit. This is how you resist fornication.

At times you may choose to satisfy your appetite for sex. Sometimes you feel that you just have to have it. You are free to do that. God is not going to throw a hammer down to stop you when you choose to give in. However, you need to think about the consequences of making that choice. There are always consequences when choosing to give in to sexual temptation. Some of those consequences are guilt, disrespect for yourself or the other person, risk of pregnancy or sexually transmitted disease, risk of getting emotionally involved prematurely.

If you keep yourself pure and resist sexual temptation, you will have a clear conscience with God, peace of mind in your life and future relationships, self-respect, respect for each other, and no worries about pregnancy and sexually transmitted diseases. You'll also know for sure that the other person is interested in getting to know you without the physical involvement.

I've heard people say, "Well, so what if we do it? God forgives." God does forgive. And, yes, we have all sinned. None of us are perfect. But the wonderful thing about God's grace is that even though he's there to forgive us when we sin, it's great to know that we don't have to sin at all. "No temptation has seized you except what is common to man. And God is faithful; he will not let you be tempted beyond what you can bear. But when you are tempted, he will also provide a way out so that you can stand up under it" (1 Corinthians 10:13). God will give you the strength to resist. He is always there in the middle of temptation to give you a way out. The phone might ring. Someone might call for help. You might get called into work. An opportunity for escape will always arise right in the middle of your temptation.

What if you do sin? What if you do fail? Well, you shouldn't stay down. You should get up. One of Satan's worst weapons is condemnation. He'll want you to feel down on yourself so you won't feel worthy to witness or live for God. When you fall, repent and ask God for forgiveness. As 1 John 1:9 says, "If we confess our sins, he is faithful and just and will forgive us our sins and purify us from all unrighteousness." Get in the word and build your spirit up for battle! What if you keep sinning? What if you can't help it? The Bible says that it's not by your might, nor is it by your power, but it's by God's spirit. You can't do it. God has to do it. You must allow him to be your strength.

Paul spoke about the struggle between the spirit man and the flesh in the seventh chapter of Romans. Verses 15–25 talk about his struggle with the flesh. In verse 24, he explains that he felt he was going crazy. Anytime he tried to live right, evil was always there with him. It's your flesh that you struggle with. That's why God sent his only son, Jesus, to "condemn sin in the flesh" (Romans 8:3). That's why you must continuously pray to him, so that the Spirit will intercede on your behalf (Romans 8:27). The Holy Spirit is your helper, your comforter. That's his job. You must employ him, and pray, so that God will move in your behalf and be your strength in the time of temptation. You cannot allow yourself to be a slave to your flesh. You have to make your flesh a slave to you, make it obey you. You do that by practicing self-control. You have to control your flesh daily, or whenever you encounter sexual temptation. Say no to your flesh.

In the meantime, use common sense; stay out of compromising situations. I know of a couple that did not even visit at each other's homes while they were dating. Before they married, they always met in public places or with other people. This was their way of staying out of compromising settings. Do what you have to do to avoid sin. Make sure your partner has the same convictions about waiting for marriage that you do.

Honor God with your body as a single person, knowing that sex is intended for marriage. Ask God to help you make a daily sacrifice to commit your body, soul, and spirit to him. Managing your sexual appetite will help you maintain your connection with God and allow you to walk in his righteousness.

How to Resist Sexual Temptation

1. **Ladies, see yourself as the jewel God created you to be.** Love and respect your body enough to know that your body is holy and should be kept for your husband only. Commit your body to God as an act of honor and worship. I've heard men say over and over, "She just threw herself at me." Women, don't test a man's desire for you by touching him or dressing provocatively for him. Allow him to get to know you for who you are. Allow him to be attracted to your inner beauty. Let him see your personality without the physical part getting in the way and clouding his perspective.

2. **Men, show yourself as an honorable and respectful gentleman.** Show her that you are a protector and that she can be safe in your presence by controlling your desires. Let her get to know you and see the strength of your character. Don't give in to her seductions. Take time to get to know her for who she really is. Look for her inner beauty. Don't be controlled by your attraction to her curves and her outer beauty. Do your part to manage the spiritual healthiness of the relationship by helping both of you stay within the physical boundaries.

3. **Make a commitment to Jesus to be faithful to him by not sharing your body with someone else other than the man he intends to be your husband or the woman he intends to be your wife.** Present your body as a living sacrifice to God. Do this by keeping yourself pure as an act of worshipping God. Commit to God by letting him know that you are faithful to him, even with your body. Your body is the temple of the Holy Ghost. It does not belong to you. It's the Lord's. Make a commitment to allow God to keep your body for your spouse.

4. **Constantly feed your spirit by daily praying and reading the Bible.** This will equip your spirit man to fight against the flesh when temptation comes. Practice keeping your thoughts pure. When lustful thoughts enter your mind, replace them with thoughts of something pure. Direct your thoughts toward God and say a prayer to him for strength.

5. **Keep yourself from looking at that man or woman too long.** Manage your thoughts by not dwelling on lustful imaginations. If there is a woman or man in your daily vicinity who tempts you to have sexual thoughts, limit the time you spend looking at him or her. Be

careful not to spend too much time looking at that person to admire their beauty.

6. **Stay away from activities that feed your longing for sex.** Try your best to avoid sexually explicit movies, songs, and books. This type of "entertainment" will only stir your craving for sex, making it harder for you to resist temptation. You have to feed your spiritual man rather than your flesh. Stay away from X-rated movies. Find other ways to stimulate your mind. Get an exciting hobby: take dance lessons, learn how to play a musical instrument, or sign up for a sports team (softball, volleyball).

7. **Don't fellowship with people of the opposite sex who don't have the same convictions you do about sexual purity.** Try to limit the time you spend with people who choose to be sexually active outside of marriage. Also, limit the time you spend with people who frequently make comments of a sexual nature. People with this type of lifestyle can make it hard for you as you try to manage your thoughts. It's like socializing with people who constantly eat junk food when you are trying to diet. You don't want to place yourself in a position to be tempted.

8. **Make a list of the consequences that could result if you participate in sex before marriage.** When tempted, remind yourself of the consequences of sex outside of marriage. Some examples are separation from God, feelings of guilt, lack of self-respect, loss of respect for the other person, resentment towards the other person for causing you to give in, emotional connection to someone you're not married to (if the relationship ends, this can be damaging), feelings of distrust of this person; and pregnancy or disease.

9. **Make a list of things you can do during those times when the temptation seems stronger than other times.** There may be time when temptation is stronger than other times. There may be times when you want to choose to give in to sexual temptation regardless of the consequences. You might feel like calling someone in the middle of the night sometimes. In those times, refer to your list and immediately take action to get your mind away from that desire. Examples of things to put on your list include taking a walk, playing some praise music, going to the bookstore to sit and read, playing some music and dancing, bowling, and jogging.

Scriptures for Resisting Sexual Temptation

Galatians 5:17 For the sinful nature desires what is contrary to the Spirit, and the Spirit what is contrary to the sinful nature. They are in conflict with each other, so that you do not do what you want.

Zechariah 4:6 So he said to me, this is the word of the LORD to Zerubbabel: 'Not by might nor by power, but by my Spirit,' says the LORD Almighty.

Ephesians 5:3 But among you there must not be even a hint of sexual immorality, or of any kind of impurity, or of greed, because these are improper for God's holy people.

Colossians 3:5 Put to death, therefore, whatever belongs to your earthly nature: sexual immorality, impurity, lust, evil desires and greed, which is idolatry.

Romans 6:12 Therefore do not let sin reign in your mortal body so that you obey its evil desires.

Romans 8:13 For if you live according to the sinful nature, you will die; but if by the Spirit you put to death the misdeeds of the body, you will live.

1 Corinthians 6:12 Everything is permissible for me—but not everything is beneficial. Everything is permissible for me—but I will not be mastered by anything.

1 Corinthians 6:18–19 Flee from sexual immorality. All other sins a man commits are outside his body, but he who sins sexually sins against his own body. Do you not know that your body is a temple of the Holy Spirit, who is in you, whom you have received from God? You are not your own.

1 Corinthians 9:27 But I discipline my body and bring it into subjection, lest, when I have preached to others, I myself should become disqualified. (NKJV)

1 Corinthians 10:13 No temptation has seized you except what is common to man. And God is faithful; he will not let you be tempted beyond what you can bear. But when you are tempted, he will also provide a way out so that you can stand up under it.

Matthew 26:41 Watch and pray so that you will not fall into temptation. The spirit is willing, but the body is weak.

Romans 8:27 And he who searches our hearts knows the mind of the Spirit, because the Spirit intercedes for the saints in accordance with God's will.

Prayer for Resisting Sexual Temptation

Oh Lord, I present my body to you as a living sacrifice. I worship you and honor you as I keep myself pure to be used by you. Please renew my mind daily and keep my thoughts pure. Guard my heart, my mind, my spirit, and my body as I live to serve you. Give me the strength and courage to yield not to temptation. Help me choose you in difficult situations. Cover me and protect me from those who would try to take what does not belong to them. Fill my cup, Lord, so that I won't thirst or hunger for what I will only crave for again. Thank you, Lord, for keeping me every day and every night. I love you, Lord. You are my everything. Amen.

Questions for Thought or Discussion

1. What thoughts occupy my mind that I need to change in order to eliminate lustful thoughts?

2. What activities do I participate in that could possibly generate lustful thoughts?

3. What relationships do I need to limit to help me manage sexual thoughts?

4. What are some activities I can begin that will help me keep my mind focused on the right things?

5. What boundaries should I set in my relationship to limit sexual temptation (if you are currently in a relationship)?

CHAPTER 14

Frequently Asked Questions

❧●❦

Before I answer some of the more popular questions asked by singles, please remember that the only true answer for your questions will come from your heart as God gives you guidance.

Here are some specific questions to ask yourself as you seek God for guidance for any situation:
- How will it affect my relationship with God?
- How will it affect my relationship with the parties involved?
- How will it affect my life in the long term?
- How will I feel about myself after it's over?
- Is it something I'll regret later?
- What were the results when I did this before?

Now, let's look at some of the questions I've heard singles ask. I have provided answers based on my knowledge, experience, and observations, but of course you may want to get professional guidance for issues requiring more advanced education.

Is it wrong to divorce?

Jesus answers this question from his very own mouth in Matthew 19:3–6, when the Pharisees came to him asking him this question:
The Pharisees also came unto him, tempting him, and saying unto him, Is it lawful for a man to put away his wife for every cause? And he answered and said unto them, Have ye not read, that he which made them at the beginning made them male and female, And said, For this cause shall a man leave father and mother, and shall cleave to his wife: and they twain shall be one flesh? Wherefore they are no more twain, but one flesh. What therefore God hath joined together, let not man put asunder. (KJV)

"Why then," they asked, "did Moses command that a man give his wife a certificate of divorce and send her away?" Jesus replied in Matthew 19:7–9, "Moses permitted you to divorce your wives because your hearts were hard. But it was not this way from the beginning. I tell you that anyone who divorces his wife, except for marital unfaithfulness, and marries another woman commits adultery."

Also, Matthew 5:32 says, "But I tell you that anyone who divorces his wife, except for marital unfaithfulness, causes her to become an adulteress, and anyone who marries the divorced woman commits adultery."

So, the answer is yes, it is wrong to divorce unless your divorce is because of marital unfaithfulness. God never intended for husband and wife to divorce. Marriage is a sacred institution and represents the relationship between mankind and God. Because of the hardness of man's heart, God made allowance for divorce, but it was not part of his original plan. In other words, except for the reason of adultery, divorce is wrong.

Am I forgiven of divorce?

John 1:9 says, "If we confess our sins, he is faithful and just and will forgive us our sins and purify us from all unrighteousness." If you have truly and sincerely confessed your sin and repented in your heart, God has forgiven you.

Will I be living in adultery if I remarry?

This is something that I recommend you speak to your church pastor or counselor about. Your pastor can guide you through what the Bible says about marriage and remarriage and help you determine how to approach remarriage. In the meantime, read Matthew 5, Matthew 19, and 1 Corinthians 7. These chapters will give you biblical insight and direction regarding marriage and remarriage.

Is it okay for Christians to date?

Yes, it is okay for Christians to date if they do so in an appropriate manner. Although the word "date" is not found in the Bible, there are a couple of examples in the Bible that you can use as good points of reference for appropriate dating. The first is how Jacob approached a relationship with Rachel. The Bible tells us that Jacob was sent by his father to find a wife. Jacob met and fell in love with Rachel. The Bible doesn't say much about how this happened. All the Bible tells us is that she was beautiful and that he loved her.

Jacob loved her enough to work seven years for the right to marry her. Although that can't officially be called dating, it does show that you shouldn't rush into making any type of commitment. You should concentrate on getting to know the other person by observing him or her at a distance without getting too involved emotionally or physically.

The reason for observing the other person is to determine if this person is a potential marriage partner. You want to observe this person to see if they possess all of the qualities vital to your spiritual, mental, physical, and financial wellbeing. Taking the time to observe without rushing into a relationship prevents you from having multiple relationships.

Another point of reference I'll use is Isaac and Rebekah. Rebekah was brought to Isaac by Abraham's servant. Genesis 24:67 tells us that Isaac loved her from the beginning. What was Rebekah doing when God provided her with a husband? Genesis 24 shows us that she was going about her daily routine. She was busy doing what she should be doing where she should be doing it. She was a faithful member of her father's household and the community. It was her spirit of service that led her to the man who took her to her husband.

Ladies, this tells you that a big part of God's preparation for your husband is for you to stay busy working for your heavenly father. In some capacity, you should be serving others and being faithful to what God has called you to do. This is how you can honorably participate in God's preparation for dating.

How long after the divorce should I wait to start dating?

The proper time to start dating is something only your heart will be able to tell. You will know in your heart when you are ready. Your heart will tell you if you have completely healed from the divorce. Whether the divorce was amicable or not, it will take time to heal. You have to give yourself time to heal emotionally. Give yourself time to get to know yourself and how you want to approach life from this point on. Get to know yourself and what you have to offer someone else. Know what your purpose in life is and how you plan to fulfill that purpose. Know your strengths and weaknesses so you will be able to show your true self to someone else.

It may take one, three, five years or more to prepare yourself for another relationship. Take all the time you need so that you will be full and complete when you go into the next relationship. You are the only one who will know when the time is right for sure.

Is it okay to have sexual intercourse with someone you love when you're not married to that person?

Sex before marriage is always wrong. Being in love does not spiritually legalize the act of sex. Being in love does seek the best for the other person. Seeking the best for the other person in a dating relationship means waiting for marriage to engage in physical intimacy. The only time sex is right is when it's with the person you're married to. There are so many consequences to having sex before marriage. All of the consequences are eliminated when you're married.

You may feel that you can't help being physical with the one you love. I talked to a man once who asked me, "Why do you torture yourself like that? You ought to go ahead and have some fun?" That so-called torture is nothing compared to the possible consequences you could suffer when you commit premarital sex: separation from God; feelings of guilt; regretful memories of people you had sex with; possibly causing distrust and resentment; artificial emotional connection to the person you had sex with; risk of becoming pregnant; risk of getting a sexually transmitted disease; risk of getting AIDS. What greater gifts can you give your spouse than the gifts of self-control and discipline, letting him or her know that you were willing to wait for marriage to give yourself to that person.

What are some appropriate things two people can do while dating to show affection?

There are many things you can do when you are dating someone to show affection. The foremost is to share the word and prayer with each other on a regular basis. This will feed your relationship spiritually and will also show love for the other person by looking out for his or her spiritual well-being. Remember, you reap what you sow. If you sow spiritual things into the relationship, you'll reap spiritual things.

On a different level, there's a list of wonderful activities a Christian couple can share found in a brochure entitled "101 Ways to Make Love Without Doing It." Some of those activities include baking cookies together, going to the library, talking on the telephone, visiting each other's family, throwing a party together, writing each other letters, going for a long bike ride, going to a movie, cooking a meal together, washing each other's cars, playing music together, and going skating.

The point is to share activities in which you show affection simply by interacting. Try to do things in a group setting and avoid private visits as much as possible. With too many private visits, there's always the chance that things will get a little hot and you will begin to feel out of control physically. Your feelings for each other may even grow so strong that at times you think, *Well, why not? I love him. He loves me. We're getting married anyway. We'll just repent later.* In situations like this, you make a personal choice. It's your choice whether you want to practice self-control. Anytime you're in a place like this, where your desire to get intimate is really strong, you still have a choice. There's always a way out.

As 1 Corinthians 10:13 says, "No temptation has seized you except what is common to man. And God is faithful; he will not let you be tempted beyond what you can bear. But when you are tempted, he will also provide a way out so that you can stand up under it." The phone might ring. The doorbell might ring. The Holy Spirit might send a conviction. Something will always happen to give you a way out of the situation. At that point, it's up to you to decide whether to go ahead and have sex or choose righteousness.

If you choose to go ahead and satisfy your desires, remember the consequences. Is it worth the price you'll have to pay? It's important to have boundaries while you are dating.

As a single person with limited income, do I have to tithe?

Giving tithe to God for the building of his kingdom is one of the most beautiful acts of worship we can give him. The income that you receive is a gift from God for you to use in a godly way.

The Bible speaks of giving generously and cheerfully. This sounds to me as though we are to give as much as we can from our heart. Giving tithe is for the benefit of the kingdom, and it just so happens that you are blessed in the process. If you are blessed with an income, you are blessed with that income to give to the kingdom. It's not yours to hold on to. It's yours to share. If you don't have an income, you can give your time by helping others.

When you give to the church, you're giving so that the ministry will have resources to minister to people. When you give to help others, you're helping that person grow in one way or another. Giving is also a part of God's plan to bless you. As you open your hands to give, God puts more in them. He wants to give you more through your giving to others and to the ministry. It returns to you to finance God's harvest, to help people who need help, to minister to those who don't know Jesus. This is what it's for. When you give to others, you are giving to the Lord.

When you give, God does not count how much money you put in the offering plate, but he *does* look at the condition of your heart. What are you saying in your heart when you give? Are you giving cheerfully? Are you giving in love? Are you giving to finance the ministry? If you are, then don't fret about how much you're giving. I would even say it's better to give less than ten percent from your heart than to give ten percent grudgingly.

If you've thought about it and prayed to God about what you should give and you feel that God is happy with what you've decided in your heart, then the amount you give is between you and God. But make sure it is indeed from your heart. Make sure that you are giving generously. You may feel in your heart as though you should give more than ten percent. God blesses whatever you purpose in your heart. He loves a cheerful giver. Sow generously, reap generously.

Do singles have a part in God's service?

Sometimes if feels as if you don't have a place in the local church because most of the ministry positions are occupied by married people. Every born-again believer has a part in God's service. In fact, the Bible says in 1 Corinthians 7:32–34 that a single person is actually in a better position to serve God.

But I would have you without carefulness. He that is unmarried careth for the things that belong to the Lord, how he may please the Lord But he that is married careth for the things that are of the world, how he may please his wife. There is difference also between a wife and a virgin. The unmarried woman careth for the things of the Lord, that she may be holy both in body and in spirit: but she that is married careth for the things of the world, how she may please her husband. And this I speak for your own profit; not that I may cast a snare upon you, but for that which is comely, and that ye may attend upon the Lord without distraction. (KJV)

When you are single, you have much more time to pray as you want to and when you want to. You have more freedom to be involved in church activities. Find the position that God has for you in your local church and use your time wisely to serve God and to serve others.

How do I deal with loneliness?

Loneliness is a spirit that visits single people often. I struggled with severe loneliness the first two years after my divorce. I couldn't seem to shake it. The heaviness of loneliness got lighter and lighter as time went by, but for a while it was rough. Some people have to have others around them at all times in order to be happy. I really don't consider myself one of those people, but I do love companionship, fellowship, and spending time with the one I love. After my divorce, feelings of loneliness would come often. I would desire so much just to talk to someone. In the midst of loneliness, I would feel sorry for myself too, that I didn't have anyone to talk to.

The best way to deal with loneliness is to have a list of activities that you can refer to when those moments of loneliness come. When the feelings come, pick up your list and do something fun. Your list could include activities such as dancing, reading, listening to inspirational music, watching a good movie, doing research on the Internet, writing a letter to a friend, cleaning a room in the house, and putting pictures in a photo album.

Make plans for yourself to occupy your time. Don't just sit around being lonely. Do something constructive. Visit the elderly or the children's ward for the terminally ill at the hospital. I have found that it lifts my spirits more than anything to visit others who need encouragement. Married people can get lonely too. Loneliness is not isolated to single people. Keep this in mind as you think about those who may need encouragement.

Is it okay to spend the night with someone as long as you're sleeping in different beds?

Have you ever heard the saying, "If you play with fire, you'll get burned"? The Bible also says in Ephesians 4:27, "Neither give place to the devil" (KJV). It's the same theory. Don't put yourself in a position to be tempted. Even if there are no intentions on either side to be sexually involved, it's best not to put yourselves to the test. It's not even good to be together late at night unless you're with a group of people in a public setting. Spending the night at someone's house is not a safe way to resist sexual temptation, even if you're sleeping in separate beds.

Is there only one "Mr. Right" or "Mrs. Right"?

I don't believe there's only *one* Mr. or Mrs. Right. I believe God allows more than one person to come your way and it's up to you to decide which one to keep. In the men I've met through the years, at least three of them told me that God told them that I am the one for them. How could this be? One of me for all of them? You see, the fact is, you will meet more than one Mr. Right or Mrs. Right. You will also meet some that the devil sends your way. You can only hope that these will be clear to you. It's important to stay in fellowship with God so that you will know without a doubt who Satan himself is sending to you. God will lead you and guide you and show you whom he has allowed to enter your life and whom you should avoid.

How much should I be willing to compromise in a relationship when looking for a husband/wife?

There are "have-to-haves" and there are "nice-to-haves." Have-to-haves are those qualities vital to your spiritual, mental, physical, and financial wellbeing. These are your necessities. Nice-to-haves are little extra benefits. These are things that add even more to your spiritual, mental, physical, and financial wellbeing. You should never compromise your have-to-haves.

For example, a good have-to-have is faith in Jesus Christ. Your spiritual being is critical for your life, so you have to have someone who believes in Jesus. Another good example of a have-to-have is someone who is financially stable. Money management is a big part of marriage's success, so you want to marry someone who is financially stable and has a job. You could even accept someone who has potential for your have-to-haves. For example, if they're not currently employed, they should at least have a solid career history. An example of a nice-to-have is a man who is tall, dark, and handsome or a woman who is beautiful with long hair and a nice shape. These are nice-to-haves because these qualities are not vital to your overall wellbeing. So, how much should you be willing to compromise? You should never compromise your have-to-haves, but if you meet someone who meets your have-to-have qualifications, you may want to consider compromising your nice-to-haves.

If you determine the person is not the one for you, you should discontinue dating. Don't date someone you know you wouldn't marry. Life is too short and there's not enough time to spend with someone who does not have your have-to-haves or who does not have the potential for your have-to-haves. Once you determine that this is not the person for you, move on.

Am I being naive to think that a true Christian man/woman won't ask me to go to bed with him/her?

Well, not necessarily. Every individual is made of flesh and bones and has sexual desires just as you have sexual desires. Hopefully, you will be attracted to each other. Physical attraction is healthy when it's managed with self-control and respect. If your dating partner is a spiritually mature person who is committed to God, she should not pressure you to go to bed. The keyword is *should* not. It doesn't mean they won't. Sometimes in dating, if there are no boundaries set, you might get into tight situations where it's hard to stop and gain control physically. At this point, it's easy to follow the desire for pleasure. It doesn't mean you or that person is a weak Christian. It just means you need to set boundaries, or, if you already have boundaries, you need to set better ones.

Is fantasizing wrong?

Fantasizing is dangerous because it could lead you into doing something that is wrong. The book of James talks about how a thought when it is conceived brings forth lust, and lust when it is conceived brings forth death. If you are sitting around fantasizing about being with someone, you are actually stirring up lustful thoughts and emotions. These emotions could become so strong that you want to act upon them. What happens if these thoughts stir up uncontrollable feelings? What will you do? You may be tempted to satisfy these feelings and desires. So, you see, it's safer not to fantasize at all.

Is masturbation wrong?

I've heard different opinions regarding this subject. Some say that masturbation is a sin because of the images you have in your head while you are masturbating. The images are of adultery, fornication, and sexual fantasy, and all are sinful. If you're watching a video, you are more than likely watching two people who are not married, therefore you are being entertained by an act of adultery or fornication. I've heard others say that masturbation is a safer option when you have uncontrollable urges, because you are not participating in fornication or adultery. I've heard people say that because you are all alone, it doesn't involve anyone else, and you're not hurting anyone, it should be okay.

The final answer is this: yes, masturbation is wrong because it denotes lack of self-control. Whether you are fantasizing during masturbation or not, it's wrong. Whether you're watching a video or not, it's wrong. Self-control is a fruit of the spirit. When you give in to the urge to masturbate, you are not practicing self-control. The amazing truth here is that your body will always crave whatever comforts you partake in.

You will always crave more and more satisfaction, just as you crave water when you are thirsty. This is what Jesus was saying to the woman at the well in the fourth chapter of the book of John. He told her, "Everyone who drinks this water will be thirsty again, but whoever drinks the water I give him will never thirst." It's so important to be full of Jesus and the Holy Spirit. When you're "full" of the Spirit, you don't hunger for anything else. It's just like eating a good full course meal. After you eat, you sit there full and feeling good. Sometimes you have to loosen your belt, you get so full. This is how you have to be in your relationship with God. Get full of him. You might ask, "How do you get full of Jesus?" "How do you get full of the Holy Spirit?" You do this by consistently praying and spending time with him. You do this by constantly reading your Bible. When you pray, just talk to God as if he's your best friend. Let him know about your struggle to remain pure and holy. Tell him that you need his help to be strong. Your body will constantly cry out for gratification because it is warring against the Spirit. The more you feed it, the more it wants.

The only way to win the battle is to feed your spirit. You won't be able to calm your flesh if you're constantly feeding it with images and music that makes you want to seek satisfaction. It will be hard for you to make righteous decisions during times of temptation if you're listening to songs about sex or if you're watching movies with explicit sex scenes. Practice feeding your spirit by having devotion time and spending time talking to God. Practice feeding your spirit by reading the Bible and listening to praise music.

Be very careful about what you watch on television and the lyrics in the music you listen to. Practice denying your flesh when the temptation to masturbate comes. Take it a day at a time. It's all about practicing self-control. Self-control is about bringing your body under subjection. You bring your body under subjection by making it your slave. Don't give in to your fleshly desires. Doing this is allowing your body to have control over you and rule you. Don't let your body rule you. You rule your body.

You can't do it on your own, though. Pray and ask God to help you practice self-control.

At what point should I allow my date to meet my children?

There's really no reason for your children to meet the person you are dating until you feel the relationship could lead to something permanent. If you introduce your children to every person you go out with, this could confuse them. Children get attached to people a lot faster and easier than adults do. You don't want to hurt your child by bringing someone into his or her life and then snatching that person out if things don't work out. They've already gone through this with the divorce. You don't want to take your children on emotional roller coasters. Wait until you know for sure that the relationship could become serious.

The point where you start considering this person for a potential marriage partner is a good time to introduce him or her to the children. You do want to make sure your relationship will be comfortable for your child. However, try to make sure everything's stable between the two of you before you introduce them to each other.

Should I accept gifts from dates?

It depends on the value of the gift and the level of the relationship. If you are in a dating relationship and you both have a clear understanding of where the relationship is headed, it's okay to accept gifts of reasonable value. You don't want to be in a position where accepting gifts from that person gives him or her the message that the relationship is more serious than it really is. If you are serious about each other, it's okay to accept reasonably valued gifts. However, if you are still getting to know each other, accepting expensive gifts may send a message that says, "I can see you want to get serious and I want to get serious too." You want to make sure the person is giving the gift as a pure gesture and not to try to win your heart. Some people are just natural gift-givers. They love to give. It's easy to take advantage of this type of person unintentionally because they so easily and frequently give. Be careful not to take advantage of him or her.

I had an experience once with a man from whom I accepted gifts. I went out with him for a couple of months when he decided he wanted to start buying expensive perfumes for me. Each week he bought a different bottle of expensive perfume. As time passed, I realized that this guy was not a good potential marriage partner, so I decided to break off the relationship. He was very angry with me for doing so and asked for all of his gifts back. He threatened me with violence if I did not return his expensive perfumes. This situation taught me to be careful about accepting gifts from men. It's so important to be aware of what the real motives are for the gifts. Are they really gifts or are they payments for a commitment they hope to receive from you?

Is it okay to kiss when you're dating?

If you are in a dating relationship with someone you are attracted to, kissing may not be a good idea. The danger with kissing is that it could lead to stronger physical activity. The reason you have boundaries in relationships, as mentioned earlier, is to prevent the possibility of falling into inappropriate activities that would cause you to fall into sin. Kissing is certainly one of those activities that you should put limits on. There are different types of kisses—a friendly kiss on the forehead, a romantic kiss on the back of the hand, a gentle kiss on the cheek. These types of kisses seem safe. However, you have to be very careful even with these types of kisses, because there's the possibility that they could lead to a kiss on the ear, a kiss on the lips, or a kiss on the neck. If you are attracted to the person you're dating, a friendly kiss could turn into a much more affectionate kiss, which could lead to something much more intimate. You don't want to risk the possibility of losing the purity of your relationship with a simple kiss. Choose the type of boundary you will have regarding kissing and stick with it.

What about Internet dating?

I believe that a reputable, credible Internet matching service is a good option for meeting someone, but it should not be your only option. I think that you should first pray and ask God to find your match for you. He knows you better than anyone and knows what type of spouse you need. I believe that as you pray and seek God for a spouse, he will send your mate to you when he is ready for you to be married.

I've heard some people say that they would rather meet someone naturally, the old-fashioned way, without using an Internet matching service. Well, I like to compare the whole Internet matching thing to a job search. When you are looking for work, you pray and ask God to bless you with a job, right? You also send out resumes at the same time. I believe the same theory applies to Internet dating. You pray and ask God for a mate and at the same time you are posting profiles on the Internet.

Of course, there are safety rules you should follow with Internet dating. Do research to find the more reputable matching services and follow all the safety guidelines. Do extensive, absolute verification before meeting anyone in person. Learn how to distinguish the people who are looking for sexual prey from those who are genuinely looking for a mate. One way to identify sexual predators is by looking at the words they use to describe the person they're looking for. If they tend to emphasize physical characteristics or use words of a sexual nature, it's a good clue that they're seeking a sexual connection. Also, if the picture they choose to display is revealing more of their body than what you think they should, that may be sign they're looking for a physical attraction. If you do decide to use an Internet matching service, I recommend you use a reputable Christian dating service that does thorough background checks and has strict requirements. One reputable service I've heard many positive reports about is eHarmony. I know people personally who found the love of their lives and married them through the eHarmony relationship service. I also know a few people who are married to someone they met on Match.com. Be careful about the matching service you choose. There are quite a few dating services that advertise themselves as Christian services that don't thoroughly screen their profiles and therefore are not as credible or as safe as others are. There are a lot of people who label themselves as Christians on the matching services also who may not be a match for you spiritually. Be prayerful and careful as you use an Internet matching service to meet someone.

Will I ever meet that special someone?

Somewhere out there, there is someone asking this same question about you. Somebody wants to meet someone like you. It is normal to want to meet someone special. And it is normal to get worried when it doesn't seem like it's going to happen anytime soon. If you're asking yourself this question, it means that this is a very strong desire for you. Well, the good news is that God gives us the desires of our heart when we delight ourselves in him. He will bless you to meet that special someone if your heart is open to whom he has for you.

Just remain faithful in your prayers to him for a mate. Continue to pray that God will prepare you for your mate. Pray for your mate as God prepares him or her for you. Continue to be faithful in the work that he has called you to do. Trust God in knowing that he is working everything out for you. Continue to enjoy life by actively participating in those activities you enjoy doing. You are bound to meet that special someone in the circle of activities you are involved in. You are bound to meet that special someone while you are busy doing what you know God has called you to do, because you are fulfilling God's purpose for your life, and he's going to send your mate to that place.

The Booster Shot

అ◆ఌ

The single life is a journey taken by many. As with any journey, there are times when the road may seem rough. There will be obstacles and barriers along the way. Even without obstacles, it's good to have guidance for our lives. We need direction and assistance with how to go about living. As singles, we need someone to talk to for advice sometimes. We need someone to help us make decisions.

The most reliable person you will ever be able to count on is someone who will stay closer to you than a brother. His name is Jesus Christ. Accepting Jesus as savior of your life is the booster shot for preparing for the single life. A booster shot is defined as an additional dose of a vaccine needed periodically to "boost" the immune system.

If you have not already done so, accept Jesus as savior of your life today. He will boost your resistance to the pressures you may encounter. He will be there for you when you need to talk to someone for guidance. To attempt to travel this road without Jesus as your partner will prove to be a very tedious. Why? Because in him is where our strength is. In him is where we get our boost for our immune system, to be protected against and have resistance to the rough times. We were created in the image of Christ. We were made to glorify him. We will never be completely happy without God in our lives. Everyone, regardless of his or her background or reason for being single, will live a much more complete life with God.

Many people spend their whole life looking for something or someone to fill a void. They try drugs, alcohol, relationships, partying, gambling, only to find that emptiness is still there. You see, it's Jesus they really need. No one or nothing could ever take his place in our lives. If you have not already done so, I invite you to accept Jesus Christ as your Lord and savior today. I encourage you to make him the foundation of your life. I admonish you to make him the source of your strength as you travel this road as a single person.

If you have not accepted Jesus as savior, you may do so by praying this prayer out loud and in your heart:

Dear Jesus, I believe you are the Son of God. I believe you died and rose again for my sins. I ask you to forgive me of all my sins. I repent of any wrong I've ever done. I accept you as my savior. I ask you to be Lord of my life. I know it is by your grace I am saved and I accept your grace in my life. I will not be condemned by any wrong I've done in the past. As of this day, I allow you to be Lord of my life. Be my strength, Lord. Thank you, God, for saving me. Thank you for accepting me as your child. Walk with me God and lead me in your paths of righteousness. In Jesus' name I pray. Amen.

Praise the Lord! The angels in heaven are rejoicing that you have accepted Jesus as your personal savior. Now you are equipped with your most important tool to help you in your single life. Please realize you don't just start a relationship the first time you meet somebody. You must get to know Jesus and build this relationship with him. You can do this by reading the Bible and praying daily. I recommend starting with the book of St. John and praying in the morning and at night. You have to stay in fellowship with God to build a strong relationship with him. Now, go and allow God to help you live a fulfilling single life!

Conclusion

❧ ♦ ❦

The antidote for a fulfilling single life is knowing and fulfilling your purpose in life. It's knowing who you are and where you're going. It's staying in touch with God on a daily basis so you'll know his plans for you. It's having healthy, meaningful relationships as you journey through life.

Remember that the greatest person who ever lived was single, and his name is Jesus Christ. One of the reasons that he had to come and live on earth was to show us how to live a victorious single life. Our aim as singles is to be like Jesus Christ. We want to be able to live a victorious single life, as he did. No, we can't do this on our own, but with God's help, we can allow him to walk victoriously through us.

Don't ever give in to the feeling that you are less than a person because you are single. Be confident and strong, knowing that if the person you aim to walk after and become like lived a victorious single life, you can too.

Be content, knowing that God knows you and knows all about you and is allowing you to be single at this time in your life. Be happy where you are right now. Embrace the fact that you are single now and that you can and will live a complete life. Keep your focus on God and what he has for you as a single. Life is short. One minute we're here and the next minute we're gone. Live your life to the fullest while you are here. Take life one day at a time. Don't worry about the future or about being single.

Don't put your life on hold waiting to get married. Don't wait to get married to buy that house you've always wanted. Don't wait to get married to travel and see the world if that's what you desire. Put your energy and passion into working for God and loving and serving others as much as you can. Take advantage of your freedom and enjoy yourself as a single within the guidelines that God has given you.

Love yourself, be yourself, and take care of yourself. Take the opportunity during this season of your life to do things you've always wanted to do but wouldn't be able to as a married person.

My desire and prayer for you is that one day soon you will look at your life and realize how good it is. I hope you will do as I did one day as

I was walking through my bedroom—sigh a breath of relief and say to yourself, "Wow, I am so content with my life right now. I am really enjoying being single."

The best thing you can do during your single days is to seek God daily for your purpose and calling in life and to be active in whatever that calling is. Trust God. He knows what's best for you. He knows how to bring the true antidote for your life.

If you're not already, start enjoying your single life today. Start by going back to the chapter "Establishing Your Individuality." Think again about what you're passionate about. Make a commitment to yourself right now to take one step toward doing something about it. Start doing what you love today. Start using your gifts and talents today.

Suggested Resources

The following are resources I have used and found to be of great help:

101 Ways to Make Love Without Doin' It. California: ETR Associates, 1991

Arterburn, Stephen, and Fred Stoeker, with Mike Yorkey. *Every Man's Battle: Winning the War on Sexual Temptation One Victory at a Time.* Colorado: WaterBrook Press, 2000

Bynum, Juanita. *No More Sheets: The Truth About Sex.* California: Pneuma Life Publishing, 2000

Carbonell, Mels. *Personalizing My Faith Membership & Ministry Profile: Combining 23 Spiritual Gifts With the 4 Disc Personality Types.* North Carolina: Christian Impact Ministries, 2006

Cloud, Henry, and John Townsend. *Boundaries in Dating.* Michigan: Zondervan, 2000

DISC Personality System—Enhance Communication and Relationships. Pennsylvania: The Institute for Motivational Living, 2002

Etheridge, Shannon. *Every Woman's Battle: Discovering God's Plan for Sexual and Emotional Fulfillment.* Colorado: WaterBrook Press, 2003

God's Little Devotional Journal for Women. Oklahoma: Honor Books, 2000

Henry, Matthew. *Matthew Henry's Commentary on the Whole Bible.* Massachusetts: Hendrickson Publishers, 2005

http://Biblegateway.com. Gospel Communications International, 1995

Israel and New Breed, *Alive in South Africa (LIVE)*. Audio CD. Label: Sony, 2005

Little Talks About God and You. Oregon: Harvest House Publishers, 1986

NavPress Bible Study. (Lifechange Series) Colorado: Navpress Publishing Group

Orman, Suze. The *Road to Wealth: A Comprehensive Guide to Your Money.* New York: Riverhead Books, 2003

Ramsey, Dave. *Total Money Makeover.* Tennessee: Thomas Nelson, Inc., 2003

Winans, Cece. *Throne Room.* Audio CD. Label: Sony, 2003

Word Ministries, Inc. *Prayers That Avail Much.* Oklahoma: Harrison House, Inc., 1997

www.ingramcontent.com/pod-product-compliance
Lightning Source LLC
Chambersburg PA
CBHW030250030426
42336CB00009B/331